Praise for Janna L. Goodwin

On *The End of the World Nothwithstanding*

"The only writer who can make Nietzsche seem funny."
—Gary Buslik, author of *A Rotten Person Travels the Caribbean*

"This wild memoir is excruciatingly honest, hilarious in its Chaplinesque escapades, and deliberate in the suspenseful nature of each story. I found myself yelling at the pages, not wanting her to make that choice, or at least look over her shoulder. As she so precisely describes 'our learned performances of cheerful compliance,' Goodwin exposes a vulnerable humility and belief in human goodness that to some could appear naïve, but to me conveys the strength of a Zen Master. She never rages against her abusers, against the weather, or the drunken driver. Instead, she reflects on the rich complexity of life and the deliciousness of being able to live inside it. This book is a beauty."
—Fay Simpson, author of *The Lucid Body*

"This is the only book I want to read, again and again, for the rest of 2021. Janna Goodwin has succeeded in writing the Best Book of the Year without even trying. There is a philosophical destination here, but the road to that destination is forever and wonderfully forking. I was thrilled to be carried along for the ride. And what message do we need more urgently these days than to laugh at ourselves at the height of our anxiety, that the best we can possibly do is to say 'Oh well—ha!' to everything, and to be reminded that we will, someday soon, be eating peaches again?"
—David Hicks, author of *White Plains: A Novel*

"Goodwin spins a comedic memoir that mines the absurdity of human experience, offering readers profound moments of insight. Because of her sensibility—self-deprecating and quirky, self-aware and intelligent—I would follow her anywhere."
—Suzanne Roberts, author of
Bad Tourist: Misadventures in Love and Travel

"Decades ago, new to San Francisco, broke but needing adventure, I began to surreptitiously follow and eavesdrop on street people who muttered aloud, explaining and justifying their lives to themselves and an invisible audience. I found a significant percentage of them to be perfectly lucid, often employing a word-perfect prose bordering on poetry. Those voices came back to me as I read this captivating, trance-inducing memoir. Goodwin exorcises painful chapters of her own past, while—and here lies her genius—commanding guffaw after guffaw from the reader, yet never diminishing the gravity of her stories."

—Brad Newsham, author of *Take Me With You*

"Janna Goodwin's writing voice is so clear, so candid, and so self-deprecating, it's hard to believe she's not sitting in front of you as you read her stories. They're not always easy, they're full of doubt and some genuinely bad decisions, but they are so very human. She wanders a lot, as people do when they tell a story, but you want to go along for the entire ride."

—Pam Mandel, author of *The Same River Twice*

On *The House Not Touched by Death*: A Medical Musical Comedy

"...a withering critique of the modern health care system (and, by extension, the entire economic establishment); an irresistible slapstick farce; an unflinchingly affecting drama; and one of the most clear-eyed looks at what really does happen at the end of life"

—Vladimir Zelevinsky, *The Boston Globe*

"Uproariously funny...There are parts of this show that Bertolt Brecht would envy, flights of mis-garbled medical jargon gone awry, songs, fables, feats of physical dexterity and mesmerizing flights of fancy. Yet always, under the frivolity and satire, throbs the heartbeat-message that no house, no human lives are untouched by death—other's or one's own."

—Larry Stark, *The Theater Mirror*

THE END OF THE WORLD
NOTWITHSTANDING

THE END OF THE WORLD
NOTWITHSTANDING

Stories I Lived to Tell

JANNA L. GOODWIN

TRAVELERS' TALES
AN IMPRINT OF SOLAS HOUSE
PALO ALTO

Travelers' Tales and Solas House are trademarks of Solas House, Inc., Palo Alto, California
travelerstales.com ǀ solashouse.com

Art Direction and Cover Design: Kimberly Nelson
Interior Design and Page Layout: Howie Severson
Cover Photograph: © Victor Zastolskiy
Interior Photographs: All images by Janna L. Goodwin except Skulls in the Catacombs of Paris by BeccaVogt, and Injury Facts used by permission of the National Safety Council
Author Photo: Michael Ensminger

Library of Congress Cataloging-in-Publication Data is available upon request.

978-1-60952-201-8 (paperback)
978-1-60952-202-5 (ebook)
978-1-60952-203-2 (hard cover)

First Edition
Printed in the United States
10 9 8 7 6 5 4 3 2 1

For Mom and Dad, who taught me to laugh at myself—
and for Michael, who makes me feel funny.

Author's Note

While I had no intention of writing a memoir—I just wanted to tell some amusing anecdotes onstage while raving about how a visit to the Grand Canyon permanently altered my perspective—I accidentally did write one.

These are true stories, and by "true" I mean that (except for the obviously imaginary sections) they happened. Even the truest of stories necessarily omits some (and emphasizes or embellishes other) stuff to make for a lively telling, and of course—as we do not typically record and transcribe our conversations with others—I've taken liberties with dialogue while adhering to the tone and quality of what I remember. Also, I engage in detours and diversions, some fanciful, some philosophical, and some factual, throughout. Where factual, I've done my best to represent subjects from wildfires to geology, cats, ships, and history accurately—but you should know that A) I might have made errors, and B) in service to a joke, I will always toss reality out the window without a second thought.

Regarding the *dramatis personae*, in several cases I've changed names and details, indicated—where the context does not otherwise make it clear—with an asterisk (*).

Table of Contents

Your descent marks your entry into a world in which planning and preparation, self-reliance, and good choices are crucial. Don't hike alone. Know what your destination will be and how to get there. Know where water is available. Get the weather forecast. Don't overestimate your capabilities. Hike intelligently. You are responsible for your own safety as well as that of everyone in your party.

—Hiking Tips, Grand Canyon National Park, Arizona

Chapter 1

You Are Reminded That Your Safety Is Your Own Responsibility

It is a beautiful summer day.

I'm traveling alone, renting a cabin at a normally tranquil spot—that's called *foreshadowing*—on the banks of the Big Laramie River at the edge the Medicine Bow National Forest up in Wyoming. You will not stumble upon Woods Landing on your way to someplace else because that's not where it is, and you've never been here on purpose. We'll have to rely on my capacity to draw you into the setting using the magic of language. Imagine a vale of cottonwood, aspen, laurel, and ash, surrounded by prairie foothills and pine-covered mountainsides. My cabin is a one-minute walk down a dirt road to a post office and a General Store with a couple of gas pumps out front. The store sells regular worms, Folger's, batteries, Butterfinger bars, and bigger worms.

Across the way is a café/saloon/dance hall that was erected—according to the informative cover of the laminated café menu—in the 1930s, by a Norwegian named Hokum Lestrum, the logs all hand-cut, perfectly-fitted to cleave together without nails, the floor supported by twenty-four boxcar springs. When the locals come here to dance, which apparently they still do on the weekends, they rebound quite a bit off that bouncy floor, which I would very much like to see. Besides that, I am up here why? First of all, I don't need a reason: I was born and grew up in Wyoming and they have to let me back in whenever I want. Second, I'm on a self-styled writing retreat. My husband, Michael, and I just returned home from a visit to the Grand Canyon that was mind-blowing and life-changing. Soon as we hit Denver and cleared out the car, I turned around and said, "Look, I have to go off again someplace on my own to think about eons and overwhelming forces and how insignificant I am. Don't watch any Sandra Bullock movies without me. I love you. Goodbye."

I am checked in before noon. I unpack and install myself: t-shirts in the dresser, six pack in the mini-fridge (cans—I'm not fancy). Ukulele on the sofa.[1] Bug spray on the counter. *Beyond Good and Evil* on the bedside table. Fishing rod by the door. In my pack are the following essentials: water, compass, gorp, and a first aid kit (Neosporin, a Q-Tip, and a Band-Aid). What I lack in skill, I make up for in provisions and medical supplies.

I scoot a chair to where I can watch the river roll by as I porch-sit, write, and read Nietzsche, then wander over to the café for a bite to eat before I settle in for the week. So why am I, a couple of hours later, standing on the porch of my cabin totally re-packed...my Fiat 500 (henceforth referred to as Vern) waiting at the ready? Vern does not literally pant, but if any car could, it would be she. They. He. It's complicated.

See, when he was brand new and my friend, Cynthia Kolanowski, first laid eyes upon his sea-foam-green adorability she cried out, as if encountering an old classmate, *Verne!*—a name spontaneously and honorably bestowed but which, for some reason, I saw in my mind as having a silent, feminine *e* at the end. It never occurred to me that Vern(e) might not be the car's name, and that does not occur to me now, but since the christening there has

---

1 On the uke, I know how to play five notes and one song called *Peaches*.

ensued no small amount of auto gender confusion on my part. When I'm driving Vern, he's a he. I can tell. I know it on the inside. When I introduce her—*I'd like you to meet my car, Verne. Verne, Jeremy. Jeremy, Verne!*—she is a she.

Yes, I do profess to my undergraduates that gender identity is socially-constructed, fluid, and a performance. I am not saying I don't want *any* trans in my car. I do—*mission* and *portation*. I just don't want to be futzing around looking for the right pronoun. So, while I am not going to run out and install a gun rack or a trailer hitch to make it clear, my mind is made up: he's a *he*. He will be raised as a he, driven as a he, and when the day comes, sold as a he. A cute, little, effeminate, Italian he.

I digress. Which according to our resident philosopher, Friedrich Nietzsche, is a sign of health, all that is unconditional being pathological.[2] I am as about as conditional as a person can be, which is why I am standing here, dithering, on the front porch of my cabin—*should I stay*

---

2 "Digressions, objections, delight in mockery, carefree mistrust are signs of health; everything unconditional belongs in pathology," is the quote from *Beyond Good and Evil*. As an aside, this is worth remembering when you are forced into sustained contact with rigid, humorless, or didactic people: you can think of it as you bite your tongue against all the wisecracks you wish you could share with them but can't because they would disapprove.

or should I go?—middle of the afternoon, scanning the sky
with a look of consternation on my face.

Consternation is appropriate. The air is hazy. There
are helicopters and small planes buzzing around overhead.
An atmosphere of let us call it *urgency* has rapidly developed, as described in the following account.

After lunch, I went over to the General Store to get me
some dessert. While I was there, three Albany County
Sheriff's Department cars came racing into the parking
area and skirched to a halt, spraying gravel and raising a
cloud of dirt, a development that—in the context of my
having recently read the café menu front to back for entertainment—was spectacularly exciting. I hung around to
see what might happen next. Unwrapped my Butterfinger.
Took a bite, watching. Deputies were here with the urgent
news that, rapidly approaching from over the foothills
across the road—quite visible from where I stood—was an
impressive column of smoke.

I did not have to be convinced of its significance.
Although I have been quite deaf in my right ear since
I had the mumps in second grade, I can see fine, and I
instinctively *get* the relationship between smoke and fire.
Not to mention, a few regulars at the café, old-timers in
feed caps, plaid shirts, and beat-up boots, quintessential

tough guys upon whom the rest of us count to remain composed at all times (they lose an arm in a hay baler, they're like, *Helen! Bring me out a bucket of ice, a towel and a plastic bag!*) moseyed outside when they saw the deputies. They appraised the horizon with nervous expressions, murmuring *Oh, no* and *Not again.*

Oh, no is what I do not want to hear certain people say at certain times. My gynecologist in the middle of my pelvic exam. The pilot of the plane I'm on as we approach the landing strip. Anybody right now on the first day of my prepaid, weeklong writing retreat.

Next, the property's caretaker, Brad*—ponytail, pecan-shell teeth, and a sizing-you-up squint—regaled our increasingly uneasy knot of onlookers with the germane tale of his own hair-singeing escape not two years ago, when this exact same thing happened only from a different direction, upon which occasion he barely got away—past blazing grama grass and exploding sagebrush, down the melting highway—using only his wits and a motorcycle. "Flames," he summed up, "was stopped right over there, where you can see 'at charred line a timber." I was able to make out a stand of blackened tree trunks less than a quarter mile away. "If this time is anything like that time," Brad noted, "we could be in trouble."

"Our boys protected us then," reminisced the General Store Lady.

"Your boys?" I inquired.

"The local volunteer fire brigade—they're all our sons out here."

This gave me pause as I reflected that, since the dawn of time, it is the young men who are called upon to put their lives on the line on behalf of the rest of us. And they do it because they're all testosteroney but also, they can't refuse because they'd look like pussies, and nobody wants to look like a pussy. Which was of sociocultural interest only momentarily: I prefer worrying to plain old thinking.

I asked one of the deputies (who appeared to be trying hard, even as we spoke, to grow his first mustache) a simple question—*Do we have to leave?*—hoping he would say, *Yeah! You're not gone time I count to ten, I'm 'onna shoot ya!* Because that would be unequivocal, no second-guessing involved.

Right, Sir! Got it, Sir! I would reply, my hands in the air. Spinning on my heel, I'd run to the cabin, throw my affairs willy-nilly into Vern and rapidly depart, doing exactly what I had been told to do by an authority figure brandishing a gun. It is enormously reassuring to believe that someone sees the Big Picture, knows what's best for us, and will take charge. Instead, though, the deputy's voice cracked a little as he replied, "That's up to you, Ma'am."

"No!" I protested, my vigor fueled by irritation at the *Ma'am* part of his sentence, *Ma'am* being an ambiguous honorific that patronizes even as it purports to esteem, construing its object as a geriatric matron who must be humored.[3] "Tell me what I should do!"

His pupils dilated. *Tell me what I should do* is not something Wyomingites—by and large Republican

---

3 Don't argue with me about this, especially if you're a man and there is no chance that anybody will ever call YOU Ma'am.

conservatives fiercely committed to a narrative of individ-
ualism and independence—tend to say or hear. He held
up his hands, perhaps demonstrating that he wasn't hiding
any intelligence that might inform my decision, mumbled
Idunno and walked away to offer zero guidance to others.

I went to my cabin, nonchalantly gathered my possessions—didn't want to overreact or worse, look like a
pussy—and here I stand, bags packed, sniffing the air, fon-
dling my key fob, and resenting the privilege that allowed
me to get myself into this situation, which might not even
turn out to be a situation at all but until I know for sure, I
am in it, and resentful.

About thirty minutes into this activity, Brad stops by to
tell me the property's now officially on alert.

"Oh," I remark. "On *alert*. What does that mean,
exactly?"

His response is earnest. "We could chill out and smoke
a doobie, but we might have to take off like bats out of
hell." He lumbers off to deliver the news to the handful
of my fellow guests—a biker couple, a family, a bearded
backpacker with a dog.

Dilemma: I have already paid for my week. If I leave,
and that fire goes tearing off in another direction or gets
extinguished, have I forfeited my retreat for nothing? Yes.

But if I decide to stay here, is it going to be possible to concentrate, write, and read Nietzsche, what with all smoke and uncertainty? And understand Nietzsche? I have my doubts.

Sure, any morality that justifies weakness and fear is an inferior one, a slave morality. I get it, just as I get Nietzsche's argument that a childish belief in a Supreme Deity limits our capacity to assume responsibility. *Duh!* Any Waldorf kindergartner can explain as much. But beyond this, I am too distracted to go deep, philosophically speaking—distracted, in part, by the fact that I deliberately chose to come to a remote location, favorable to creative introspection under ideal conditions but inconducive to wireless signals. Which was brilliant right up until the huge, scary fire started, when a gal needs to be able to get onto Wikipedia. Not Google, which is where our worst fears go to mutate due to the fact that only those who have had appalling experiences bother to share them, in graphic detail, on websites that appear when you search for—I don't know, say *centipedes in Hawaii*.

A couple of years ago, my cousin, Kim—who lives on Oahu but didn't have room to play host—came to hang out for the afternoon with me and Michael in our theretofore perfect vacation condo smack on the beach in Haleiwa. The three of us were sitting around, sweet Pacific breezes wafting in through the sliding doors, mai tai flowing (it was as if my glass kept filling itself). Life was good. Until Kim wondered aloud if we had noticed any centipedes scuttling about.

"Centipedes don't exist!" I scoffed.

"Actually, we have them all over the island." She held her fingers eight inches apart. "They're about this long, and they move really fast." She disclosed having recently hacked one to bits upon finding it skittering up the side of the entertainment center in their actual living room: "So I grabbed a hatchet—"

Michael recapitulated, "You keep a hatchet near your television."

Confirming this with a nod, Kim gazed up, her big, brown eyes expertly searching the ceiling.

"Are you telling me they can *drop on you from above?*" I wanted to know, because that really seemed like too much.

What I shouldn't have done—after Kim left and I was alone in the condo with just Michael and the internet—is, I shouldn't have sneaked out to the lanai with my hand-held device and conducted a Google search for centipedes in Hawaii. I regretted it, and not just for the rest of my vacation. I will regret it for the rest of my life.

———

Wikipedia, on the other hand, as any college student can tell you, is where we go to obtain *knowledge*. Once on it, I learn that wildfires move at a speed of more than six miles an hour in forests and fourteen miles an hour in grasslands. Woods Landing, as I explained earlier, is in a grassy, high plains valley at the edge of a forested mountain. That is what, nine hundred and thirty-eight miles an hour. Or not; I majored in theater, not pyro-dynamics. Anyway—if I can now get the precise coordinates and boundaries of the blaze, take into account the topographical features between it and me, and ascertain the likelihood (and potential velocity) of wind, then armed with numbers—and mathematics—I can begin to calculate my chances. But I keep losing the signal. For Pete's sake, all I want to know is, should I kick back—drink an ice-cold Titan IPA, pen a lyric essay on the Grand Canyon, fingerpick the one song I know how to play on the ukulele—or should I run away?

Provided with data, I am capable of responding appropriately (even with equanimity) to any number of scenarios. Keeping things in perspective is why I never go anywhere—including on this trip—without my copy of the 2012 edition of the National Safety Council's popular *Injury Facts*.

Which invaluable publication, alas, has limited use at the moment. Oh, sure, I can look up *Fire*, where subcategories such as *Smoke Inhalation* and *Burns* draw my attention to an array of possibilities. But I want to be online is what I'm saying. Only the network, WoodsLandingGuest, is unresponsive. I'm walking around the property with my phone, waving it as if trying to attract the attention of a passing spaceship: *Come take me home!* I read somewhere that for more bars you should swoop your phone around above your head in a figure eight pattern. I don't think it works. I do it anyway. Zilch. Accordingly, it comes to pass that the aspect of my trip I most looked forward to—being out of touch, out of range, and away from it all—leaves me reliant upon speculation, face-to-face interaction, and word of mouth. The speculation is vague; the faces are unreadable, and the word is *Idunno*.

Don't get me wrong, I am surrounded by perfectly decent fellow human beings: the afore-mentioned Brad. The General Store Lady. The deputies, a bartender, and *oh!*—this multi-talented sixteen-year-old who, up at the café, took my order, made and served me a fine green chili burrito, cleared my table, rang me up, and gave me correct change. These are the sorts of capable, competent professionals to whose judgment surely one might entrust one's wellbeing.

Yet when I say to Green Chili, "What I mainly need to know is are we all going to die?" he answers, after considering the question, "I think so." At the look on my face, he adjusts this to, "Oh, you mean because of the fire. Well, we all live out here, and we have not been ordered to evacuate."

"Precisely!" I affirm, then—as he subtly backs away from me—continue. "This is the center of your world. I can see you all setting up those big, yellow, FasTank emergency water reserves and running with your pumps and hoses to the river, which leads me to believe the situation here is—for all of you—dire. That said, I am a stranger passing through, one who might avoid loss of life, limb, and property. So as regards the peril to me personally, what would be your best guess?"

I wish that I did not suddenly see myself through his eyes but it is too late; I do, and what I see is jumpy, wimpy, and bothersome.[4] To repair this fresh problem which regards shame due to unwanted self-awareness, I volunteer to assist in the fortification and defense of Woods Landing. Words to that effect come right out of my mouth, making me an even worse person because I do not mean them.

---

4 Jumpy, Wimpy, and Bothersome will be the names of the dwarves in the fairy-tale version of my life.

Now I imagine myself missing my chance to get away, trying to look brave, and opening up a fire hose only to be blasted, by the unexpected force of the water, thirty feet backwards into the river, where I crack my skull on a rock. I can see it clearly: me drowning, not even doing something genuinely useful but only *pretending* to do something useful. They have to stop what they're doing, fish me out, and resuscitate me. Meanwhile, Woods Landing burns down around us. *That woman is the worst thing that has ever happened to us!* laments the General Store Lady, and so begins my local notoriety. I end up, after Hokum Lestrum, an item on the cover of the café menu, a sorry episode in an otherwise proud history. Diners shake their heads in disgust when they come to my paragraph.

I am therefore relieved when Green Chili responds to my offer, "No, there's nothing you can do here. We got a whole training and procedure and everything. Go on down to your cabin. You'll be okay." This last part (which I, as an adult, probably ought to be telling *him* by way of comfort and encouragement) is sweet, in spite of the fact that we both know he's mainly trying to get rid of me.

Back to my cabin I go, thinking *Maybe this is an opportunity. If anybody ever needed to find peace with being on alert, it is I.* Writing is a centering activity. I take out my Pocket Guide to the Grand Canyon, my notebook, and a pen. Open a beer. Sit down. Recall what brought me here. Begin to write. This, from my journal entry that day, page 23:

> The Grand Canyon is nearly two hundred and eighty miles long. In some places, it is deeper than a mile. Seventeen million years ago, the waters of a great river established a course through what we now call the Colorado Plateau as it was being uplifted by tectonic plate colli-sions. This effected erosion on a magnificent scale that continues even today, exposing nearly two billion years of the Earth's geological history. The oldest human artifacts in the canyon are eleven thousand five hundred years old. People migrated to the Western Hemisphere at least four thousand years before that. Our remains have been found elsewhere that are estimated to be one hundred ninety-five thousand years old.

Dinosaurs went extinct around sixty-one-million years before humans appeared on earth, having been in existence for something like ever. The Vishnu Basement rocks—that's the layer at the very bottom of the canyon—could be 1.75 billion years old. Here is what I find myself wondering: my life span thus far is what percentage of those vast ages? Let me just work that out in my head. Okay, got it: the answer is .000003428.

For a long time, I try to visualize this infinitesimally small number, imagining it first as the single beat of a bee's wing, then as one bird chirp, or as the momentary glint of light on a ripple in the river. Sometimes, when there's nothing else to be known and nothing to be done, a little context goes a long way.

When at last I raise my eyes to behold the mountain, it is obscured by a thick haze. The sun, beginning to set, casts a glow like nothing I have ever seen. But for the distant throb of chopper blades, all is still. Under the porch, a lone cricket sings. I don't know what's coming, but of course, that has been true every minute of my life.

Chapter 2

Mind the Abyss

Michael and I have a new toast. *Oh, well!* is what we say when we lift our glasses. To mitigate the quality of resignation, I like to add a cheerful sound at the end: *Oh, well—HA!*

This is a replacement for our previous toast, *To the living and the dead!* which we started using after barely avoiding being mangled in a tragic wreck on Highway 50 in South Central Colorado. I was passing a Kenworth cement mixer, heading up a long incline, a two-lane highway with a center passing lane. Michael sat in the passenger seat gazing off to the north. He had just asked me if that was Pikes Peak you could see in the distance, and I was ignoring him. A Volkswagen Sirocco had come flying over the crest of the hill at a high rate of speed, angling right at us, drifting across those double yellow lines as if they were made of nothing more than paint and good ideas.

I braked, shouting *nonono!shitshit!nono!* which was not a prayer—I do talk to God, on occasion, but this was no more than a vehement denial of our fate—and ducked Vern back behind that Kenworth at the exact moment it protected us from the impact and flying debris. Driver of the Sirocco[5] was killed. No one else was injured. To this day, my favorite kind of truck is cement.

That is not a story about heroism—of which I have none as far as I know—nor about my quick reflexes, which I *do* have. Because of how I am strung, you should replace the word *quick* with *startle* in almost every case

For instance, say Michael and I are in different rooms of the house and he wants to enter the room I'm in. A considerate man, he yells out *Warning! I'm down the hall!* then *I'm approaching the doorway! I'm almost there!* I hear his footsteps arriving. *Here I am!* he states trepidatiously—and still, when he comes into view I jolt violently, emitting a yip like a nearsighted, coked-up Chihuahua who catches

---

5 I found the notice a few days later, in the Canon City Daily Record. Her name was Deanna. The cause of her car barreling, headlong, down the wrong side of the road remains a mystery.

a glimpse of itself in the hallway mirror. This is just one of many features of our marriage that make it exciting, and living with me an adventure.

But this is also not about that. It is about how anything can happen at any time, and usually doesn't but sometimes does. *WAIT*—*!* is what it ought to say on my headstone, because that will surely be my last, conscious thought. I don't want to be buried, by the way—I'd rather be cremated—but a headstone would be nice so it can say *WAIT*—*!* People can come visit me and laugh. Which will make me happy. Except, I'll be dead.

Speaking of which, have you been to the Paris catacombs? Are you in for a treat! You pay for your ticket and they give you one of those miner's hardhats with a lamp on the front. You sign a waiver stating that you understand what it's going to be like down there, affirming that you want to go anyway. Then you descend a tight, spiral staircase, down, down, down—one hundred and thirty steps—with all the other helmet-wearing visitors clomping ahead and pressing upon you from behind.

At the bottom is a tunnel. The guide provides historic highlights: excavations, explorers, escape routes, and the cautionary tale of poor Philibert Aspairt who, long ago, got lost while trying to find the famed Chartreuse liqueur rumored to have been hidden in the catacombs by Carthusian monks. Philibert only brought *une bou-gie. Une!* I don't want to be all critical of other people's ill-advised escapades, but let us consider whether (or not) one candle is a good idea for descending into the bowels of the earth looking for something hidden that no one else has been able to find. In my opinion, any adventure that ends with your remains being discovered eleven years later could have used some rethinking.

Anyway, following in Philibert's footsteps only to the point at which they vanished, onward you now trudge with the others, through the gloom and stifling heat, toward your destination. At some point during this lengthy sub-terranean tour, it occurs to you that you are protected from the crushing weight of the city above by only a few remaining columns of rock. But you can't be all *Ho là! Excusez-moi! You know what? I did not realize it until right now, but this is not going to be the activity for me. I'll just be waiting back up on top of the ground.*

Because, no. Sometimes, as we all know from having been born, returning the way you came is not an option. Here, the corridor is narrow. There are people crowded around you front and back, blocking the way up and out—and behind them, the next group is already descending those stairs. Closely on both sides yawns the occasional abyss, pointed out by the guide, way up front, who periodically cries out in scornfully inflected English, "On your right is anozer abyss. Do not fall into it."

As a simple American tourist who now realizes you're at the mercy of the situation, your best course of action is precisely that—*Do not fall into the abyss*—plus move forward, stay in line, keep breathing. Try to not make a spectacle of yourself. Eventually, you all come to a small opening. The lintel is inscribed with something memorable, which I forget. Guide says that you are about to enter a sacred place. *Defense de fumer,* he sniffs. *Do not smoke a cigarette.* Then *pop!* In you go. And there are bones as far as you can see—on and on, lining the walls of the passageway like cobblestones, curving from the soft, dirt floor into the low ceiling: human pieces, human parts.

By the 1700s so many had died over the centuries—especially during times of plague—that corpses, having a tendency to pile up and re-emerge, became a problem, floating in the swampy ground of the cemeteries, a well-known public health *faux-pas.* Until one day, some genius had an epiphany: *Sacre bleu! Why we do not srow all of zese bodeez down, sroo ze oles of ze ventilation—to ze old mining toonnels?*[6]

Which came across as an excellent idea. So for the next twelve years, under the direction of Louis-Etienne Hericart de Thury—which will be on the quiz, along with how fast wildfires can travel and a True-False question about snakes (don't worry, that's coming up)—the good citizens of Paris arranged all those anonymous crania, vertebrae, tibiae, fibulae, scapulae, femurs, and ribs into patterns: circles, waves, rows and hearts, all set into a sea of elbows and knees. You can reach out your hand to touch the cool, ambivalent skulls as you pass, and for a long time, you pass—and for a long time, you caress—until your hand knows it is made of the same stuff. *Oh, well—HA!*

---

6 Sacred blue! Why we do not throw all of these bodies down through the holes of the ventilation to the old mining tunnels?

Chapter 3

Fraidycat

Lini Vega* and her husband Raoul* were heading off to Europe for two weeks and needed somebody to house sit.

They were not wealthy, but prosperous, fortunate, and talented. Theirs was a domestic arcadia eight miles outside Boulder, Colorado, tucked away at the upper end of a winding canyon road with an easterly view that opened, from between spruce-covered mountains on either side, to the descending foothills and expansive, smog-blanketed plains beyond. Impressively, they had designed, built, and landscaped it all themselves. I had been up there once, at a party, and remembered its deck, wildflowers, vistas, spacious great room, cathedral ceilings, tall windows, and comfortable furniture, and now I raised my hand, waving it frantically in the air. We were sitting around a table at the Dark Horse at the time with three or four other friends, so raising my hand was unnecessary.

"I'll do it," I said, calming down as soon as I was called on. "I'm totally available." I was between gigs and needed work. Getting out of town and up into the higher elevations for two whole weeks sounded more than appealing. Others in our group—whose eyes had, like mine, lit up at the prospect—quickly checked their calendars and, alas, discovered normal adult reasons that they could not compete against my abundant free time, so I won the job. I did not request details; I was in.

Months earlier, I had arrived in Colorado after nearly a decade spent on the East Coast—Boston, New York, and the Pioneer Valley of Western Massachusetts—where I had wrapped up a lengthy series of peripatetic educational endeavors, co-founded a theater company, assumed the role of temporary executive director for an arts organization that was two lean months away from folding (and then, it had), been cheated on and dumped by my significant other, and seen four people I cared about—two beloved teachers, a classmate, and a dear friend—succumb to AIDS all within two years of each other. I was worn out.

My parents and my brothers, Mitch and Matt, all lived along the Front Range and up into Wyoming. After years on the other side of the country, I looked forward to hanging with the family. Mitch and I have always liked exploring unfamiliar neighborhoods and going from coffee shop to coffee shop, talking about whatever comes to mind, drinking joe until it's time for brewskis. That was exactly the sort of activity in which I wanted to engage for a while so, since he called Boulder home, that's where I wound up, too.

At age thirty-six, I was living paycheck-to-paycheck thanks to my career, which was ridiculous. You can do theater for fun, or you can, as I did, take it seriously. You can turn it into a professional identity. You can get an audition, get an agent, get hired, get into a union, pay your actual and metaphorical dues. You can participate in what you think are top-notch, transformative projects, all of them ephemeral. You can write grant proposals and scripts; live in shared quarters, in colonies, or on the road, in motels; you can make solo work, make ensemble work, make your friends and family go see your next show—but (this is one of the industry's Best-Kept Secrets) you cannot make money. Not really. Maybe if you started out with money and know the right people. Maybe as a designer— but not as a playwright, director, or performer. Not enough to pay off student loans, buy a mattress and box springs, or obtain health insurance. Not even if you live in New York, unless you are extraordinarily lucky, and certainly not if you've turned your back on that singular hub of live theater to reside in Colorado. So while you are coming to terms with past experiences and pivoting toward new, different ones—perhaps feeling dazed, perhaps stuck— you bartend catered events. You cover the switchboard at the Boulderado Hotel while the real receptionist is on maternity leave. You write press releases for the Colorado Shakespeare Festival, and you take on a variety of other odd jobs.

Of this latter description, house-sitting for Lini and Raoul sounded like a paid vacation. On the spot, right there at the Dark Horse, I started fantasizing about how I'd use the time—not to study for the GREs, read *Coding for Dummies*, or update my resume, all of which would have been forward-thinking. No, it turns out, I am an incorrigible playwright—screw pivoting!—and there is nothing a playwright relishes more than a quiet retreat with naught to do but take care of some house plants, stare off into space, and talk to ourselves out loud, unheard and unobserved, trying out dialogue. I could hardly wait. My lips started to move in anticipation.

"Oh!" said Lini, "You're not allergic to cats, are you? There's a kitten."

I am not allergic to cats or to anything, as far as I know, except for penicillin, and how I found that out is another story for another time. I only mention it here because the more people who know about my allergy, the more likely it will be that someone—perhaps *you*—will quickly apprehend what's wrong with me, should I one day ingest penicillin by mistake and find myself red, blotchy, and swelling, unable to choke out an explanation…and the more likely it is that you will save my life, administering the antidote which, for the record, according to the internet, is *epinephrine*. Just do your best to recall that one thing, and come prepared. Thanks in advance.

Not being allergic to them doesn't mean that I am a fan of cats. I am aware that by acknowledging this truth about myself—neither boasting about it, nor criticizing anyone else for their cat-love—I nonetheless open myself up to all kinds of opprobrium. There was a time (most of human history) when a person could articulate a feature of their own psychology or personhood, such as *I think cats are just okay*, without being subjected to insults and death threats. I fear that time has passed.

Our family was not petsy. Still, as a kid, I was allowed to have a parakeet, Tweety, of whom I was terrified: she pecked when I reached inside her cage to feed and water her, and screeched when I changed her paper. The pecking didn't hurt but seemed as if it ought to. When she got out of the cage, which happened a few times, she'd first flutter around my head, to make sure I was sufficiently cowed, then would aim for the ceiling or an open door or window. Once, when Tweety escaped, my father followed her from tree to tree and yard to yard carrying a ladder until, with the help of a neighbor (it was a two-man job, not counting the several, highly engaged spectators), the fugitive was captured in the branches of a tall cottonwood, brought down without injury, and re-caged. Tweety died a short time after this, of natural causes.[7] I next tried raising a rabbit, Blackie—I was a literalist denominator—who chomped down on fingers with enough force to break the skin; who could gouge you with one, powerful swipe, and who would not abide cuddling. When I write here that Blackie had to go, I mean nothing sinister: he was donated to a farm.[8] Fleetingly, when I was thirteen or fourteen, we owned a beagle who farted incessantly and pungently for her first (and only) week in our care, then—in full heat— ran away followed by a pack of seven male dogs, all of whom had been gathering at our back door for days, hoping. Ultimately, we located her and quickly gave her away to other, better people.

---

7 Records will show that I was in school at the time. I can't vouch for Dad's whereabouts.

8 Or, so I was told.

Fraidycat

Regarding cats, my acquaintance has involved mainly living with roommates who owned them, always in pairs. I have noted that it's never just Muffin or Whimsy; it is Muffin and Whimsy, Ted and Brian, Tiny and Tubbs. One cat seems to either subdivide into or otherwise cause—who can say how it happens?—a second cat. (So convinced was I of having cracked cat protocol that, upon hearing her addendum, I'd inquired of Lini, "A kitten? Just the one?" but she'd brushed off my implication with a breezy, "Yep! One's enough!")

I also know that cats will urinate on your possessions. I am told this is merely a "marking of territory" but can't we be honest? The cat is flipping you off. I know that cats are totes full of themselves. That they will sit in windows, heckling irritated squirrels through the screen, for hours. That they will walk across your newspaper or chest and park there, as if all other places are occupied. With ramrod tail pointing to the sky, they will display their anus, right up in your face. They can be ingratiating when they want something but are otherwise haughty and dismissive. They might keep you amused for hours, batting at fake mice on strings. Some enjoy curling up in your lap, which is when you throw caution to the wind and allow this thought to cross your mind: *What a pleasant pussycat with its very soft fur and its contented vibrations!*

———

Lini introduced me to my room, spa-like quarters with sumptuous white bedding and a meditation alcove featuring a tatami mat, bamboo plant, and burbling table fountain. There was an en suite bathroom with a whirlpool tub and sauna. I couldn't wait for her and Raoul to leave, but first she had to brief me on my few responsibilities.

Outside on the wrap-around deck, a mind-boggling profusion of planters and pots lined the railings—different sizes and shapes, spilling over with varieties of mountain-hardy flowers; there was a hanging garden, too—all of which, Lini explained, I should water and deadhead early every morning. *Deadhead*, I repeated, nodding as if I understood what she meant. I am not someone who is afraid of looking ignorant or who holds in my questions, but there was something about her manner that suggested *of course you, like all civilized people, are a conscientious deadheader*. I did not wish to disappoint, nor to make her change her mind about entrusting her petunias to my care. Fortunately, she started deadheading unconsciously as we wandered around the premises, so I was able to pick up the basics.

I did, in that moment, feel the difference in our lives, along with a blush of shame at not having figured everything

34

out as well as she had. I wasn't jealous. I wouldn't have traded places with Lini—charming, good-looking, and flourishing as she and Raoul both were—because I was okay with who I was, but also I had seen movies where people swap bodies and lives, and there are often complications. That said, here we stood, approximately the same age, and she seemed so much more grown-up. I made a mental note to cultivate flowers in pots when I got back to my real life, and to deadhead them.

The Vegas' private, dirt drive descended through a terrain of tufted grasses, columbine, larkspur and black-eyed Susans, broken up here and there by rocks and small boulders so aesthetically grouped that it was impossible to tell if they'd been placed there or had occurred naturally. The air was scented with terpenes. Nothing reminded me, except by omission, of vocational muddles, existential dis-illusionment, or economic tensions; I felt lighthearted and hopeful as Lini led me on a hot, unprotected walk[9] down to the main road, where the Vegas' postal box sat clumped with ten others, the only indication of the secluded homes that must have surrounded us. I was to go here in the after-noons to collect their mail, after four o'clock when the

9 Not that I'm trying to argue that absolutely everything can poten-tially hurt you, but know that at seven thousand feet, the sun can. UV exposure increases by four percent for every thousand feet.

postman had passed by. It would become a routine. I started to envision the tranquil shape of my upcoming days.

There was one more thing, Lini said, leading me back up to the house. "Luka."

It wasn't that I had been looking forward to meeting the kitten, but I was surprised that we hadn't come across him yet. "He's shy," Lini told me, calling out *Luka!* in every room, which filled me with doubts about her legitimacy as a cat owner: shouldn't she know that, when a cat hears its name, it is required to act as if it has a far more important caller on the other line?

Down in the finished basement was a TV room, an office, and a large storage closet. When Lini touched the light switch, a shadow flickered in a dim corner behind the entertainment console. "There he is!" She went to him and picked him up. He was gray, bigger than a ball of fur, long-limbed, an adolescent.

"Awwww," I said.

"He's just over four months old, and he's—oh!" I had tentatively extended a hand to Luka, whose eyes—glazed with loathing and alight with hostility—enlarged to the shape and size of pennies. The kitten hissed ferociously, stiffening and twisting as if possessed, in Lina's arms, whereupon she rapidly set him down with an adoring titter. "He's going to have to get used to you is all. Let me show you what and where he eats."

The Vegas would be mostly traveling in Spain—trekking, off the map—so I could expect to hear from them only once or twice. As I had told them I planned to stay at the house full-time, with no trips to town unless absolutely necessary, they were leaving me a thoughtful stash of soup, crackers, and nuts in the pantry, and milk and cheese in the fridge, upon which surface was affixed, by a CU Buffs magnet, a list of emergency contacts. When Lini pointed it out, I took note without much interest. Why would I need emergency contacts?

Raoul poured Luka a bowlful of food, and while the kitten was distracted, the couple rolled their bags out the door to their SUV. Standing at the driver's side window, I remembered something.

"I have an old friend who's coming through Denver this weekend," I said. Josie* was a massage therapist who toured with big-name musicians. Her current client was headlining at Red Rocks. "Is it okay if she comes up and stays with me for one night?" I had raved to Josie, in our last phone call, about my short-term luxury digs and, since she would have twenty-four hours off, she wanted to visit.

"Of course, yes!" I was assured. Was there anything else? There was.

I had expected the subject of compensation to come up by now, but it hadn't. I needed either an advance, or to know how much I could count on so I could budget my way through the month. I was down to fifty dollars in the bank, ten in my pocket, and the gas in my tank. Rent, on the cramped duplex I shared with a housemate in Boulder, would be due before the Vegas got back. I decided to spit it out.

"Is there any way I could get a check for maybe half?" When both Lini and Raoul looked bewildered, I stammered, "Or, even a couple hundred would be great." Their blank expressions did not brighten to comprehension. "Kidding!" I cried, holding my arms wide as if to embrace them, their house, the view, the entirety of the Rocky Mountains, the sky and the universe beyond. "I should be paying you! You guys! You should have seen your faces!"

Lini looked like she might cry from relief; how awkward, if I'd been serious! We all had a good chuckle, and away they went.

He will try to get out the door, Lini had warned me. *Do not let him. He'll get lost or eaten; there's wildlife all over the place. He won't have a chance.* As I was coming back inside, he not only tried but succeeded, flying past my ankles before I could block him. The rest of the afternoon was spent as follows: I called Luka's name. This was as productive as it had been earlier, when Lini had done it. I scanned the exterior of the house. I went down the hill and checked between rocks, behind trees. I called his name. I put his food and water in front of the door from which he'd escaped. I walked down the road. I called his name. I could not believe I had lost the Vegas' kitten within thirty seconds of their departure. Around me were hundreds of thousands of acres and more of wilderness, stretching in all directions, unbounded. A kitten could be anywhere. He was, thankfully, in a tool shed twenty yards from the house, under a bench. He was okay. I had him. Now, all I had to do was pick him up and get him into the house.

Three hours later, I felt like Foreman at the end of his notorious '74 *Rumble in the Jungle* with Ali, defeated, humiliated, and a bit melancholy. All exposed skin was sunburned. My arms, shins, and calves, and the tops of my feet in their flimsy sandals, were not shredded (*shredded* would be hyperbolic) but significantly lacerated. I had not written any plays. Instead, with the kitten temporarily shut inside the shed, I had hunted around for resources, coming across a cache of cardboard booze cartons in the basement storage room. These, I had deconstructed and flattened, duct taping them together into a flexible, two-by-six-foot wall that I used to corral Scaredy-Claws—it improved my state of mind to silently mock him—when he ventured from his lair, lured by a dead bug I'd found and tied to a length of dental floss.

My lower extremities were sheathed in protective newspaper, wrapped and fastened, also with duct tape: improvised gaiters. On each hand, I wore a grill mitt. I'd envisioned lifting Feral Cactus, gently but firmly, in both mitts and transporting him to and through the side door of the house. Once inside, I would kick the door closed before letting him go. I had everything prepared: he was trapped, the door to the house was propped open, and all I had to do was get him through it, but my gear—I shall refer to the outfit I've described as *gear*—made it impossible to execute the swift, painless, and efficient move I had pictured in my mind. I couldn't seem to keep the corral braced while simultaneously positioning myself to extricate the target using both hands. As anyone who has trained for this scenario knows: one hand wearing a grill mitt cannot pick up a kitten.

It occurred to me that I could inch the entire corral-kitten situation southward to the threshold. I then opened the one side so that Jabberwock could discharge directly into the house.

Whew, I thought…because I had no idea.

Fraidycat

————

Twitchy Barbed Wire stalked, hissed at, and attacked me throughout the evening. I did not remove the gaiters, so I was able sit at the table or counter and eat, but reading or writing anything was out of the question. The moment I forgot myself, crossed a leg or shifted, the kitten launched itself at me in a wild, murderous rage. Resting on the sofa in the great room invited an ambush, so no. I did realize that I could close myself in the basement to watch TV downstairs, but watching TV wasn't why I was here, and nor was being confined to a basement. For his part, Mean Feet wouldn't go near the basement door. Getting him down there would cost me another several hours and probably an eye. Also, I didn't feel that it would be right, morally speaking, to imprison him in isolation. So, hoping we might still salvage our relationship, I engaged him with a toy, speaking and moving gently to signal that I meant no harm. His fur standing on end, he arched his back, a Halloween caricature, and spat at me.

When I went up to bed—early, after only several glasses of chardonnay—Freaky Painmaker bounded—or rather, corkscrewed, airborne—into my room.

It was a long night.

———

That Friday, Josie got herself from Denver to Boulder, where I collected her at the bus station after signing myself up with a temp agency. I was not a one-trick playwright: I could greet people, type, control an automobile, speak French, and (new skill) deadhead a garden. Were I to be hired soon to do any of these things, I would have to commute back and forth from the mountains, about half an hour each way, but if I weren't, I would be in trouble with my housemate and our landlord come the first of the month—or to put it another way, I'd be the cause of inconvenience to them and they'd think poorly of me. A damaged reputation is not easy to repair. I knew this, because I already had a reputation for 1) having to pee too frequently to be much fun on a road trip; 2) never cleaning inside a refrigerator or behind a toilet, and 3) being the opposite of laid-back. The first two were and are justified; the last is bogus.

Cell phones would soon utterly transform all of our communicative lives but were still in the future, which is to say that Josie and I had not been in constant touch. There had been a call or two, but for coordination purposes only; we were not caught up. I wanted to hear about

42

the present tour, which had taken her from coast to coast and was in the final stretch. Josie's strong, capable hands had kneaded the knots out of some very famous muscles, and her current client was one of my favorite singer-songwriters. Disappointingly, there was no celebrity gossip; Josie was nothing if not discreet. I was, however, thrilled to learn there'd be a free ticket waiting for me at the box office tomorrow night. Today, we would barbecue us some fish and vegetables and sit on the deck, watching the valley below darken, the stars come out, and faraway Boulder begin to twinkle.

The whole way up the canyon, Josie entertained me with anecdotes about a new romance and backstage antics, so there wasn't a chance to fully disclose what we were walking into. Or, I mean, there were plenty of chances— Josie is not an incessant blabbermouth—but I thought I might sound melodramatic. Let's just say that I withheld some stuff.

As we pulled up to the house, Josie went, "Wow! That is awesome!"

"It's a hellhole," I said.

In preparation for my guest, I had maneuvered Porcupussy to the basement door, where I'd gotten him to the top of the carpeted stairway. That had enabled me to tape the corral around the doorway. He was sequestered, apart from the upstairs living quarters but not really closed off. His litter box, scratch post, food, and water were all accessible. I was satisfied with this solution, at least for now. Until today, I had not left him unattended for long; I'd talked to him, dangled things in front of him to bat around, and had (regrettably) offered a trembling hand to see if he'd let me touch him, which nope. I had left the lights semi-dimmed. I had put classical music on the stereo and played it constantly. After Josie's visit, if things continued as they'd been going so far, I would clearly have to do more, maybe involving professionals, as I couldn't keep a kitten in a basement for twelve more days.

Talons was plaintively mewing when Josie and I walked in.

"Stop!" I said—or possibly screamed—when Josie went over and reached down for him as if he were a regular kitten. "That is not a good idea."

She laughed and—with the confidence of someone who grew up with pets and magically connects with them all—got him by the scruff, as if firmly letting him (and me) know who was in charge. She lifted him to her arms. I flinched, but Satan let her hold him.

"Who's this?" she asked in a baby voice. "Who IS this adorable little boy? Who ARE you?"

"I cannot urge you emphatically enough—" I began, but then we both heard it: *purring.*

I could tell that Josie might never again look at me with the respect I'd theretofore been accorded, and I felt sorry about that but remained ill at ease. She was being too cavalier. She did not—could not possibly—grasp what we were dealing with here.

We sat in the great room, where I explained how the past forty-eight hours had gone: an hour of watering and deadheading in the morning, a walk for the mail in the afternoon, and the entire rest of the time, day and night, entertaining, contending with, and evading the kitten, its teeth, and its claws. The whole time I was describing his behavior, Josie caressed him and Lunatic stared at me, unblinking, more tightly-wound than any creature—other than myself—I have ever encountered. I so, *so* wanted Josie to put him down, behind the barrier, so that we could, ourselves, unwind, but she was committed to demonstrating that this charming cutie was nothing at all to be afr—

"MOTHERF*CK*R!" Josie yelled as the thing in her arms went berserk. In an instant, her arm and hand were deeply scored, her chin nicked, and Luka had fled. A lot of other words followed the initial outburst, but you get the gist.

The next morning, in spite of washing and antibiotic ointment, Josie awoke in pain, her hand and arm red and swollen. I dialed two of the emergency numbers on the refrigerator: the Vegas' veterinarian—to whom I told everything, and who had some common-sense suggestions, most of which I'd already tried—and their nearest neighbor, who I asked to please (carefully) look in on the kitten, as I had to rush one of its victims to a clinic and would not be home until quite late.

Josie and I spent the morning in my car which, keeping things interesting, was running low on fuel. It is an hour and a half from the canyon to South Denver, where we had located an Urgent Care facility that would take Josie's insurance, and which had agreed to see her right away. After a long wait and a short appointment, I spent my last ten bucks on gas, and we headed out to Red Rocks, another eighteen miles.

There, I blissfully hung out—far, far from the Vega house—in what has to be the best place on the planet to sit and do nothing or to see a concert: a natural amphitheater, its breathtaking realm contained by massive outcrops of 290-million-year-old rock, the eroded remains of the Ancestral Rocky Mountains, tinted by iron oxide, the same compound that gives rust and blood their hue, and Colorado its name. Inhabited or visited over thousands of years by Paleo peoples, considered sacred by thirty-two indigenous tribes, once known as Garden of the Angels then Garden of the Titans, Red Rocks is revered by locals, and is fondly recalled by anybody who has attended a performance there. This summer evening, the temperature was warm; the crepuscular light, soothing; the scent of weed, seductive; the show, fantastic. It was possible to believe that everything would sort itself out, because life was good.

I briefly saw Josie and her bandaged hand and arm afterwards. We hugged. I apologized (although…was this my fault? I was distraught, but was I culpable?) and we parted, for she was off to the next city.

Eventually, I would find out that, in the aftermath of the incident, Josie—whose livelihood depended upon her hands and her robust health—had been forced to quit the last two weeks of the tour (infection, stiffness, weakness, illness, shots)—but that night, it seemed she'd be fine.

Fully encased in newspaper and my new favorite product, duct tape, I managed to write on Sunday. I sketched out scenes for what I was then calling *Undiscovered Country*,[10]

---

10 It was later developed and produced, by me, Pilgrim Theatre, and Ko Theatre Works, as *The House Not Touched by Death*

a new script I'd begun toying with a few weeks back. What I had in mind would be a musical farce about mortality, communication, and what was starting to be referred to as the "medical-industrial complex"—with which inter-sections I'd become familiar of late, notably during my recently-deceased friends' individual and collective hos-pitalizations. I was approaching structure randomly, writ-ing scenes as they occurred to me. One story I wanted to tell involved an old woman, Katie Fino, who, at ninety, frail, and in the throes of a health crisis, is ready to let go, but her daughter and medical team insist upon keep-ing her alive. Nothing in the play would be literal; the characters would be upbeat, cognizant of and vocal about their thoughts, fears, and wishes, even during their critical events. The dialogue started out fine:

> NURSE: Now, Mrs. Fino, what do you want us to do if your heart stops?
>
> ILYANA (KATIE's daughter): You give it a bump with one of those shockey things! Don't they teach that in medical school anymore?
>
> NURSE: No, I don't mean that we don't know what to do technically. I mean (to KATIE) do you wish to be resuscitated?

KATIE: No.

ILYANA: Yes!

KATIE: No!

(*Teeth bared, ILYANA hisses, flying at her mother with her sharp fingernails*)

ILYANA: Then fine! I hate you! Die! Die! Die!

I crossed out the last line, broke for a mug of chamomile tea, then started working on a new scene—this time, two friends, Jesse and Louis, coming to grips with Louis's AIDS diagnosis. Jesse is listening to Louis's fears, empathizing as he wrestles with the specter of his own mortality.

MUSIC UNDER

LOUIS: Do you think there's an afterlife?

JESSE: Oh. Yeah, I do.

LOUIS: How about a before life?

JESSE: Well, we gotta come from someplace.

LOUIS: Because, I'm wondering, if there's a before life, do we get any counseling? Pre-season instructions? Like, when we're just a gleam in our parents' eye, is there some Big, Old, Kind

Voice that says to us, "Hey, spermatazoa! Listen up, Ladies!"

JESSE: Yes! I'm sure there is!

(*Speaking in a Big, Old Kind Voice*)

"I just want to make sure that you all understand the conditions that you will face out there. There are wars and fires! Floods and famine! Sinkholes, sociopaths, and viruses, too! So consider what you are about to do, and what it will surely cost. Before you go, I will tell you, you may suffer. You may cry. You may often feel afraid, and you will ache in the pain of confusion. But-

(*Singing*)

You will eat peaches; you'll see suns set—

You will taste honey from the field,

Though you may receive the sharp sting of the bee—"

(*Teeth bared, LOUIS hisses, flying at JESSE with his sharp fingernails*)

———

Monday, the temp agency called. On Tuesday, I should report to my assignment by eight in the morning. I rose at dawn, deadheaded and watered, and donned my gaiters. I let Luka upstairs so he'd have the run of the premises. I set out food and water, corralled off the front door, stepped over the barrier, and once outside, removed the gaiters. I locked the door, leaving the key where the neighbor—with whom I'd secured an arrangement—could find it in order to perform a midday check-in. I drove to Boulder, to an office park, to the headquarters of the custom neon sign company where I would be answering phones for a few days. I was hastily trained, met the staff, toured the workshop floor—the production of custom neon signs is, by the way, equal parts fascinating and mind-numbing to watch—and worked until one o'clock, then stopped at my bank, withdrew forty dollars (perhaps you have calculated how much I now had left) and drove back up to the house, arriving by two.

I phoned my landlord to give a heads-up that my upcoming payment would almost certainly be late, to ask that my housemate not be blamed, and to request leniency and forgiveness.

I phoned the vet, to set up an appointment for Luka, as I now felt sure that he was defective in some way that needed addressing by a more qualified individual than myself. The vet would see him tomorrow—but I'd be working again, so we decided I'd bring him by as soon as I got off. I made it clear that I could not pay for this visit, describing the circumstances and disclosing just enough information about my own indigence to feel exposed and abashed. The assistant assured me that they knew the Vegas and would bill them, but if I could get Lini or Raoul to give her a call, it would be super helpful. *It would be super helpful*, I respectfully corrected her, *if they would give me a call.*

With a start, after hanging up, I realized the plan upon which we had just settled would mean keeping Luka in a carrier—assuming I could locate a carrier, and assuming I could get him into it—at my workplace, for hours. Was this better than leaving him alone at home for another day? Was it worse? I calculated time, mileage, remaining gas, and remaining money and decided I had no choice.

I phoned the temp agency to explain my problem. They suggested that I contact the neon sign company. I did. My supervisor there told that everyone there had children, pets, and untidy lives, and that it would be fine.

The Vegas called that night.

"Janna!" said Lini's voice, tinny and distant, yet familiar and welcome. "How's the playwriting going?"

I had penned five short, disconnected scenes, all of them ending in abrupt and senseless violence. "Great," I replied. "How's your trip?"

"Great," she said. I wondered—if Lini meant *great* in the same sense that I was using the word—how bad things were in Spain. "And Luka? You two hitting it off?"

"Your flowers are happy," I told her, because this was true, and it was good news. Then, I delivered the bad: *Your kitten has been stressed-out, angry, and off his rocker since the moment you left, if not before. I have to go into town daily to earn my rent. I can't afford to stay here for another week, and nor do I want to. Luka needs something I can't give him.*

I did not mention the whole Josie debacle, but did say that I'd made an appointment for Luka with the vet tomorrow, and that Lini needed to call them. I felt my stomach tighten as I related all these things. Lini sounded dismayed. I could not read whether this was on the kitten's account, mine, or both. She apologized that this had happened. She said she'd call her sister, who would probably agree to come tomorrow and to stay. I would be able to go home; my work here would be done. After that, I stopped listening.

———————

I watered and deadheaded the next morning, then went to work. Luka came with me: I'd cornered him with the carrier, eased him into it with the grill mitts, and managed to get us out the door by seven-fifteen.

He was either too stunned to protest, or else he liked the containment because, sitting there on a corner of my desk, he was preternaturally still. Employees stopped by to coo and poke at him through the metal grid. One woman put her nose right there, even though I advised, "I would not put my nose right there if I were you." The kitten had those gigantic, crazy eyes again, but I felt he was holding everything in, amassing power, reserving his enraged frenzy for when it would most count, at the vet's, perhaps, when they opened the cage.

"What a *schweetheart!*" lisped the nose woman cloyingly—the closest I will ever come to being a mother with a new baby, specifically, Rosemary.

The vet and his staff would examine Luka and keep him overnight, under observation, to see if they could identify anything physically going on. If not, they had some behavioral interventions. Another cat might help, it was suggested, at which I had to refrain from shouting, *And if I know that much, why don't Lini and Raoul?*

When I got back to the Vega house—cat-free, hoping to write for the remainder of what could turn out to be my only peaceful afternoon in a week—Lini's sister, Ada*, was waiting for me in the kitchen, crushing the last of my hopes. She had a sinewy, "can-do" thing going on that you see mainly in Boulder's female athletes, the ones who—on Saturdays—bike up to where they can climb a fourteener, rappel down the other side, raft back home, and go for a run before noon. She was acting the tiniest bit like I, not the kitten, might be dangerous. I wondered how Lini had represented our scenario, mine and Luka's, because based on Ada's demeanor, I doubted that the account had been sufficiently grounded in examples.

She would take it from here, she said. Other than asking, *Have you actually met Luka?* (she had not), I didn't say much. I had packed most of my things this morning, put away the grill mitts, laundered and folded the bedding, given the house a final once-over, recycled my gaiters, and erased any other evidence that I'd ever been there. Except for one thing.

"What's that?" asked Ada, pointing.

I explained the corral: how to fold and secure it around the kitten should he get outside or become nettlesome in a less-than-optimal part of the house. I showed her how to affix it to the basement doorway. Instead of admiring my ingenuity, she kept murmuring snarky things that were supposed to sound friendly, but weren't—*Yeah, I'm pretty sure I can handle a kitten*—so I didn't mention the grill mitts. I could tell that, like Josie, she knew exactly what she was doing.

Chapter 4

Reality

While it is everything essayists, naturalists, adventurers, and poets allege it to be, nature can also suck, which I know personally because I read books. By which I mean I watch television. Our favorite show in the so-called reality genre is set in nature, and believe me, it is no picnic. It's called *Naked and Afraid*.

For the uninitiated, it goes like this: two strangers—a man and a woman—have auditioned for and been selected to endure three weeks in some wild, far-off, isolated place—jungle, desert, island, swamp—without any clothes. Having won this amazing opportunity, they now get to do that while being videotaped. Each is allowed to choose and bring a single implement—knife, machete, fishing spear, et cetera.

The show provides contestants with transportation, a small burlap bag (in which to carry a digital camera for video diary purposes), and a smudge of genital pixilation. Besides these affordances, they're completely on their own except for a 24-7 camera crew which you, the viewer, are supposed to forget exists.

During their self-inflicted ordeal, the intrepid pair faces all kinds of challenges and travails.[11] In the end, they make their way—still naked, still afraid, but now also famished, bug-bit, sunburned, cold, wet, sick, and pissed-off—to a site from which they are, at last, extracted and whisked home to civilization to recuperate.

In follow-up interviews with the producer—back home, wearing puka shells and playing Frisbee with their dog on the beach—winners usually claim to be super glad they did the show. Apparently, we cannot know who we are—or of what fiber we are made—until we have scratched three feet into the dirt with bare hands to a source of water, built a yurt out of vines tied together with strands of our own hair, devoured a giant cockroach for

---

11 Whether or not they have sex with each other is always a question, but one left mercifully unaddressed by the show. Usually, mutual tolerance rapidly curdles to mutual loathing (e.g., to her, he's a controlling sexist; to him, she's a controlling bitch) or one of them gets so sick they can't contribute anything or takes the *I'll just lie here and not move for three weeks to conserve energy* approach, while the other finds stuff to do like hunting slugs and complaining, and because none of that is hot, viewers don't think much about copulation.

protein, and been documented in these, our exertions. An aside here, but relevant in the larger scheme of things—as previously noted: on my personal List of Terrors, giant cockroaches are Numero Uno.

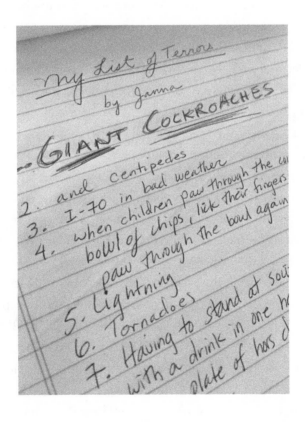

my List of Terrors
by Janna

GIANT COCKROACHES

2. and centipedes
3. I-70 in bad weather
4. when children paw through the w... bowl of chips, lick their fingers, paw through the bowl again
5. Lightning
6. Tornadoes
7. Having to stand at sou... with a drink in one h... olate of hors d...

Surviving is harder than a person might think. Life is everywhere on this planet—if nowhere else in the universe—and *it all wants to eat you*. Some life dines on you from the inside out. Other life nibbles at your feet and between your toes, gets in your crevices. Some stings you or sucks your blood, or crawls in your nose or your ear, or takes up residence in your hair, or lives on your scalp, under your nails, between your teeth. It gets in your lungs, knocks you down, stands on you, rips you apart, swallows you whole, and licks its chops.

I'm not trying to gross us all out here, but do let's try to assess our condition honestly, with courage and acceptance: as we consume, so are we being consumed. Is that so hard to admit? It is. You have to be careful not to think about it too much, which is difficult when you watch *Naked and Afraid*. Frankly, I don't know how we're still here as a species, given how delectable we are.

The awful truth about our biological existence acknowledged and exposed nowhere more evidently than on *Naked and Afraid*, I still had THE BEST DREAM EVER IN THE HISTORY OF DREAMS after binge-watching the show five nights in a row. *I am not making this up: my dream was a complete episode.* The guy of the couple (whose name, in my dream, was Jeff) had chosen to bring along a tape measure as his survival tool. The woman (Stacey) toted a machine gun as hers.

After searching for hours, the only water they were able to locate was a small mud puddle, around which feature they decided to construct their shelter. The enterprising Jeff measured out an expansive footprint, spending several days figuring out the dimensions, making sure they'd have plenty of headroom, and even planning out a kitchen, a yoga studio, and a tennis court.

Stacey took on the role of provider, first shooting and pulverizing a bird, leaving nothing but a red mist hanging in the air, then *rat-a-tat-a-tat* reducing a grizzly to Swiss cheese. Sadly, neither she nor Jeff could figure out how to get at the bear meat without a knife. In an ugly moment, hungry and frustrated, she taunted him to cut the carcass open with his asinine measuring tape—a hostile exchange that he experienced as emasculating.

As he recorded an offended video journal entry, he noted *sotto voce* that their trials and tribulations were exacerbated by the fact that…and here, rather than finishing his sentence, Jeff panned from a selfie of his own wan countenance to show us, the viewers, the nearby camera crew's hygge, L.L. Beansy glampsite, where the show's producer, director, camera operator, and medic all sat around a portable picnic table, enjoying a meal of roast duck and figs, yards away from where Jeff and Stacey lay on their insect-infested bed of sticks. On the crew's table were goblets of wine, pitchers of beer, bottles of water.

The producer belched loudly. Instantaneously, from right beside Jeff—who was still recording—there exploded a volley of machine gun fire. In the silence that followed, Stacey justified her hair-trigger reaction: "I heard a sound." Stacey and Jeff checked to make sure the entire crew had been eliminated (it had) then proceeded to survive, for the remainder of my dream, by eating all the food and drinking the water and wine left behind; sleeping in the crew's tents, and playing Angry Birds on the crew's iPhones. In the end, they were extracted not by the show's usual methods but by a SWAT team in a Blackhawk.

I breathlessly recounted my dream to Michael immediately upon waking, while it was still vivid. I am not sure that he fully appreciated it.

Then, I couldn't stop thinking about improvements the actual show might make in the future. For example, why keep putting the contestants on some desert island or in the jungle? Why not leave them, naked and afraid, in the Lufthansa terminal at LAX, or at the Mall of America? I'm not saying that wouldn't be problematic. I guess you'd have to ban money, cell phones, credit cards and driver's licenses. Contestants would not be allowed to access the internet or get in touch with family or friends. They'd still have to be naked. See how they do for twenty-one days. Or, maybe they'd just have to last for an hour. I don't know! Pay me a salary and I'll figure it out.

In real reality, there is a man who survives, in the alley right behind our house, within about eight feet of our garage door. Although we inadvertently serve as his audience, there is no television crew recording his many hardships, and no prize awarded for resourcefulness or stamina when he makes it from one season to the next.

A cardboard tarp and a sleeping bag establish the center of his base camp. Scattered (or arranged) for several feet in all directions is a circle of detritus, stuff he's foraged: ketchup packets, empty bottles, milk carton. Cereal box. A purple sock. Enigmatically, a can of Static Guard. All this, which he pulls from a number of nearby refuse bins and strews about, forms a perimeter that suggests the boundaries of his territory. You don't go clean up, because he has claimed the rubbish as his own, so it just gets wetter, fruitier, filthier, and more plentiful as the days and weeks pass.

For hours at a stretch, Oscar rants and raves—yes, we refer to him as Oscar, after the fuzzy, anti-social muppet of Sesame Street. Calling him The Violently Enraged, Delusional Paranoid Schizophrenic would be more accurate but it's not as affectionate. Thus *Oscar* kicks his shopping cart over, picks it back up. *AAANGHHH!* Kicks over our recycling bin, picks it back up. *AAANGHHH!* He paces up and down. He hollers. A lot. His least favorite thing is our dumpster, which he calls a goddamn whore and tells it to go to hell.

Once recently, I was out there depositing our weekly, stuffed Hefty bag when Oscar came hurtling at me, yelling murderous, misogynistic epithets. He is wiry and powerful-looking; his brown hair detonates in all directions, and the whole display is quite striking. I hurried inside, fully aware of the suffering that Oscar must endure every day, thinking *You know, we all have our stories.* And in mine, I've had my fill of being accosted, harassed, menaced, and otherwise beset without my assent. I don't want to be intimidated. I don't want to be advanced upon when I am minding my own business, taking out my garbage. I don't want to be threatened when I'm merely fulfilling my civic duty, just trying to be a good (enough) person.

If I sound defensive and peevish, this is because I have a friend, Naomi*, who will not permit me to have my own experience of Oscar. I can't express to her my feelings—about his presence, his rage, his glee at scattering trash, and his high-decibel maledictions—without coming off as the lesser person, the undeserving, privileged whiner in the scenario. When I tell an Oscar story (like the time I took out the recycling, was harassed and vituperated—C*NT*SSF*GG*T!¹² –and, while hightailing it back into the garage, tripped and fell) I am to express only compassion for his plight.

"Poor guy," she sighs.

"Yes," I say, because I truly agree. "And yet."

---

12 His abuses, when intelligible, can include some creative and bewildering juxtapositions.

"Have you asked him if you can help?"

"What? No! He's like one of those superfast zombies."

"Let me come check him out. I'll see if he needs to be connected to services."

"No."

Naomi is not a social worker, she's a Pilates instructor. This is the same friend who—when I told her a few years ago that I'd been charged at by a snarling dog while taking a walk—wanted to know if the dog was okay.

Here is what I have learned about Oscar from other neighbors and from the cops. He isn't homeless; he lives nearby, in an apartment, with a relative, for whom I have sympathy. She's afraid of him. She tells police to arrest Oscar if they catch him committing crimes and otherwise to leave her and Oscar alone. She can't do anything about him, he won't take his meds and that's that. The community officer of our local precinct warned me NOT to attempt to befriend him (I had asked if I ought to try that), explaining that some cheerful do-gooder down the block was once assertively kind to Oscar, who then proceeded to show up—for weeks—at the dude's front door at two in the morning, demanding to be let in. Another person had apparently introduced herself and tried to insert herself into Oscar's care network, whereupon he'd started waiting outside her house and following her. He is shunned by homeless tent campers—including the bike theft ring, the chronically down-on-their-luck, and the addicts who populate the recesses of the neighborhood—since he tries to rough up the women and gets into fights with the men. He is a force of nature.

So no. I'm not going to get to know him. I think I already kind of do.

Chapter 5

Then They Come Toward You

My parents and I took a road trip to Kansas not too long ago. Let me just say that—until the last few hours—this was a way better time than you might imagine upon hearing the words *parents*, *road trip*, and *Kansas* in the same sentence. We have a blast together and frankly, we had no idea what was in store for us.

At first, it was all fun and games. In Nebraska we stopped at Red Cloud to look at—let's say it all together—Willa Cather's house![13] When we got to where Dad grew up in Brown County, Kansas, we paid respects to the Goodwin family gravestones on the hilltop, surrounded by blue sky and emerald fields. My father explained corn.

We saw all the attractions in Hiawatha. Grain elevator. Pool hall. Dusty genealogical office where they were so

---

13 I am not being facetious. I love Willa Cather.

nice, they dropped what they were doing (what all they do when we are not there) to locate archival photographs of my dad's big farm family, taken back in the '40s and '50s.

Next, we visited Aunt Mitty, a little old lady who lives by herself in a three-room house in White Cloud, population one hundred and seventy, a charming if disintegrating town located right smack on a muddy bank of the flood-prone Missouri River. Aunt Mitty, who is legitimately related to someone in the extended Goodwin clan but is everyone's aunt, possibly even yours, has known my dad since he was a sprout. When she greeted us at the door—after not having seen Dad for I'm guessing thirty years—not only did she recognize him instantly, but she was all *Gary Gordon Goodwin! You all come on in and take a load off!*

Aunt Mitty's arm was in a sling. Her hand and wrist were wrapped in a serious bandage. This occasioned the following explanation: a few days earlier, she was folding sheets and towels, right there in the kitchen, when she uncovered a big snake lying, coiled, in the laundry basket.[14] She figured it must've been attracted to the warmth of clothes fresh off the line. Which is only one of two things that you will learn from me about reptiles: while they do not care for direct heat, snakes like feeling cozy, just like you. Snakes are people, too.

---

14 *IN THE LAUNDRY BASKET!!!*

In her account of things, Aunt Mitty picked the serpent up by its tail or latter end, whatever you call that part, and was swinging it around over her head so as to sling it out the back door when it sank its fangs into her hand. Which pissed her off so, with her other hand, she grabbed a nearby hatchet—apparently, my cousin Kim is not the only family member to keep one within easy reach—and chopped that bad boy right in two. She flung the pieces into the yard. Then, she went and got a neighbor, who drove her thirty-eight miles to the hospital in Hiawatha.

All this she recounted with a complete lack of astonishment or bravado—even with a tone of *This isn't much of a story, but*—the way you or I might casually tell of swatting an annoying fly.

I admit that, sitting there in Aunt Mitty's living room a few feet away from the site of the incident, I was disinclined to sink back against the cushions of her sofa. And while balanced on the edge, I kept lifting my feet off the floor, holding them by sheer willpower in the air, occasionally grunting.

That night, we drove up to the Camp Rulo River Club for a catfish dinner. Next morning, we headed home, and this is where it *all gets real*. Mom is driving. Dad is up front with her, eating cold, leftover catfish and fries straight out of the Ziploc bag in my mother's purse. I'm in the back seat, looking out the window. I can see, in the distance, this cloud. It seems to be pretty far off, just a dark, little cube floating over the unmitigated emptiness of the Great Plains.

And I don't like it. I don't like it one bit. Soon, I feel compelled to make a comment: Hey, *look at that cloud.* Nobody pays any attention to me. Remember that.

After a while, we come to a T in the road and make a left. We are right outside of Otis, Colorado. That cloud has expanded into a massive, gnarly, dark ceiling, and now, I'm squeaking and hissing.

The methods I use to express agitation and to influence people's behavior were all developed when I was three and have not matured since then. They include:

Squeaking
Hissing
Bellowing orders
Whimpering
Gasping
Clenching the muscles of my pelvic floor
Picking at my cuticles
Forgetting to breathe
None of these has ever been effective.

Around ten years ago, on a family hike in the White Tank Mountains outside Phoenix, I deployed them all at once. Dad stood still on the trail ahead, waving me and Mom closer. "It's a rattler!" he cried. Never have I seen him look more delighted. I watched him approach to within a couple feet of this mound of reptile, where he squatted down for a closer look.

I, contrastingly, retreated to a more reasonable quarter of a mile away, from where I roared my instructions—"DAD! NO! GET AWAY FROM THAT SNAKE!"— which failed to induce any change in his posture or location. I went through my whole repertoire: I squeaked, whimpered, and clenched to the point of traumatizing my Alcock's Canal, an anatomical structure you have never heard of until now but, take my word for it, it's not something you ought to squeeze. Dad merely regarded me with a bewildered countenance, then glanced suspiciously at my mother, no doubt thinking to himself, *I cannot possibly be Janna's biological father.*[15]

---

15 What Dad knew and I did not was that snakes can't strike targets farther away than 2/3 their body length. That is a thing I was surprised to learn. A native of the Wild West, I nonetheless always assumed that rattlesnakes coil tightly so they can spring through the air at their victims, unconstrained in their propulsion. I did not consider the physics and now I do. Thank you, Wikipedia, and that wraps up the second of my two snake facts for you.

Friends, there is no climax to my conniptions, ever. Because the terrible things that happen—and terrible things do—are unrelated to anything that I suppose is about to occur. Nonetheless, I seem to be hard-wired to predict their cataclysmic inevitability. And frankly, let us observe together that our mediated world loves stirring us up. It happens when we least expect it. *Wonder what the temperature's going to be later on today. Think I'll check the Weather Channel website. Let me just scan the—YIKES!* Next to the forecast, there appears a grainy photograph of a pretty bride holding a knife, recoiling from something. The headline reads *SHE CUT INTO HER WEDDING CAKE AND FOUND THIS.*

Weather.com and its advertisers, the entertainment industry, the twenty-four-hour news cycle—not to mention religion—get something essential about me and I daresay about you. It is this: the remove of anticipation from dread, excitement from fear, thrills from chills— that remove is not a separation, it is a verge, and we are verge-dwellers.

So, naturally, I click that bait, and so do you. Because we cannot *not* find out what was in the wedding cake.[16]

---

16 Mold: plain, old everyday mold. Unacceptable, sure, but no giant, flying, toxic, Bolivian tree slug, which is what we all thought it was going to be.

What I am saying is that, after more than half a century of knowing me, my parents—by the time we are on our way back from Kansas (you remember Kansas? The cloud?)—are used to my lively interpretations of everyday phenomena. They just start humming or turn up the radio real loud. But then, I kid you not, a thin, twisty finger DOES STRETCH OUT FROM THE SKY TO THE GROUND. Imagine my excitement. I have my iPhone ready, which is why the heart-pounding drama that follows was recorded for posterity. I don't come off too well in the video, but I'm sharing it with you[17] because I told you so. What you can see in the distance—thrillingly shot by me from the back seat of the car, looking out through the front windshield—is the descending funnel. What you can hear, unfortunately for me, is the conversation. The scene begins as I turn the camera on, catching my own self, mid-outcry.

ME: —because we're heading into a tornado! That is going to go down to the ground, and here we sit. It's *going down to the ground!*

My parents barely respond, my mother driving calmly and relentlessly onward, my father almost certainly enjoying the flashes of lightning. "GO BACK!" I urge. "Jesus,

---

17 If you saw the footage yourself, you would agree that I sound like a reporter covering Godzilla's rampage live.

you guys! Go the other direction!" A pickup truck ahead of us can be seen pulling over to the side of the road.

ME: When people pull over—! It's going to the ground! It's going to the ground!

DAD: (*Unperturbed, as if describing a cloud in someone else's life, or in a novel*) We're not going anywhere near it. It's about six miles to the north.

ME: And then they come toward you!

DAD: (*Brightly*) Like snakes!

Rain is hammering down. The wind picks up as we pull into Otis, population five hundred, seven blocks long. The town's tornado siren goes off. We come to a stop sign, where I lose the rest of my composure, which wasn't much to begin with. I roll down the window of the Avalon and— to a fellow wearing a Jayhawks t-shirt, sitting serenely on his front porch—appeal loudly, "DO YOU HAVE A BASEMENT!?[18]" Other than staring, he's unresponsive, which I take to be a *no*. I feel I ought to wish him well, however, so as Mom accelerates I shout, "GOOD LUCK THEN! GOD WILLING, MAY WE ALL LIVE TO SEE ANOTHER DAY!"

Rounding the corner, we pass a church—no fortress, but sturdy-looking—and with a cry of "STOP!" I leap

---

18 Implying *and may I get into it immediately?*

from the car to assault its front door with my fists, wailing (as much as I hate to admit it now) "WHAT IS THE POINT OF A LOCKED CHURCH?" My parents are now scrunched down in the front seat, far more discomfited than frightened. Dad's hand is over his face, and he is shaking his head. I am utterly beside myself. I insist that we must find shelter immediately. Giving in at last to my hysteria, Mom pulls into a parking space next to a modest eatery. She and Dad start to slowly—nay, reluctantly—unbuckle themselves, as if we are the first bashful guests to arrive at a soirée. I don't even wait to help them from the car. They're in their late seventies, not frail but slight: each weighs less than a pumpkin. The wind is howling around us, blowing every which way, the car doors flapping out of control—and my attitude is, more or less, *You guys are on your own!*

I yank at, then pound upon the door of the diner. *Push!* reads a conspicuous sign. When I do that, I am able to enter effortlessly. What do I see inside but chaos: people crowding into a root cellar at the back of the kitchen or cowering together in the booths, weeping and trembling. Nah, I'm just messing with you. What I actually see is folks eating lunch. Enjoying their grilled cheeses and tomato soups, shooting the breeze. I overhear *Goin' up to Lincoln on Saturday to check out a used—*

The speaker falls silent and everyone, it seems, looks up at me. I must appear to them as Oscar appears to me when he comes raving down the alley: deranged, foaming at the mouth, all sanpaku eyes and flailing limbs. Behind me, the door swings open again and a gust hurtles my parents inside. They are soaking wet. Dad grins and addresses the now-expectant crowd, holding out his arm in my direction as if ushering me onstage to accept an award.

"Good afternoon, everyone. This is my daughter, Janna. She's alarmed by the weather."

Tornado siren? Still going off but I guess, in Otis, *What tornado siren?* Now I just want us to fit in, please; to pretend that we came here for coffee. We spot an empty booth and sit. A handsome young father—he looks like a farmer—excuses himself from his table (his wife and children smile at me from across the room) and threads his way over to us, squatting down next to me and taking my hand. "It's going to be okay," he says reassuringly. The waitress brings over menus and three mugs, which she places around the table. Without asking, she fills mine from the *orange* pot.

Then They Come Toward You

Chapter 6

And I'll Obey

I was fast asleep after a long day of stretches, scenes, songs, swordfights, *ports-de-bras*, and character work at the National Shakespeare Conservatory (or NSC, as we alums refer to it). Things were good.

Yet, in the dank, second-floor studio sublet I shared with my boyfriend, Greg, I lurched awake, shivering and numb. I had either forgotten how to breathe, or I was having a coronary. "I need to go to the Emergency Room," I pronounced. When you have no money for cabs, a four o'clock a.m. trip to Beth Israel from Tompkins Square means a teeth-chattering walk through an eerie Manhattan, where all you hear, against faint, distant sirens and the low, eternal hum and throb of electricity, is raw hacking and heaving from deep within alleyways, and the scampering and squeaking of rodents.

"Just a panic attack," determined the impassive E.R. nurse, who saw a lot worse (probably every few minutes) and no doubt wished that I—a sober, twenty-something theater student—had sucked it up at home and stayed away from the front lines where they dealt in life and death. The word *just* in the nurse's mouth was both insulting and reassuring. By the time we got back home, around dawn, I felt fine. Soon, the incident seemed like it hadn't really happened. But panic would come after me again in a few months, when its appearance, duration, and severity would be disabling.

I *loved* NSC. Loved my teachers, loved my new friends, loved being in a studio all day long with other actors, and loved having my bumbling attempts to act critiqued by a master. Today—even as I tiptoe around the innumerable sensitivities that seem to have become points of pride among college undergraduates—on occasion, I'll tell my students about this period in my life, and about how much it meant to me to have teachers with enough confidence in my robustness to shove me—often ingloriously—out of my comfort zone. To treat me *not* like a delicate *fleur* or precious vase, but rather the way a good coach treats a boxer who shows promise.[19]

---

19 In the movies, I mean; I have no history with actual boxing coaches.

Rigor, a kind of buzzword in actor training, was my middle name. With zeal, I took to the task of becoming a better actor. I was willing to fail—and to undergo frequent losses of face—in service to that goal. I'm surprised when friends don't get it. Some, for example, are appalled when I appreciatively recount one of my fondest—and most complicated—memories: playing Miss Julie in a scene from the eponymous play by Strindberg. My triumphant downfall, my awful success, occurred during Scene Study class.

Miss Julie, if you don't know already, is the seductive but wretched daughter of an aristocrat. She has a brief, torrid affair with her father's household servant, Jean. Complexities develop—desires meet obstacles and there is conflict—and in the end, Julie implores Jean to command her to commit suicide. *Help me now!* she pleads. *Give me orders, and I'll obey like a dog. Do me this last service! Save my honor—save my name! You know what I ought to will, but don't will. Do you will it and order me to accomplish it.*

I was performing badly—gamely attempting to take on language and ideas that were way beyond me—and Casey Kizziah, an adored faculty member, was directing. The whole class watched. *Give me orders, and I'll obey like a dog.* I was an adult—one who had experienced flirtation, sex, even trifling debauchery—but at heart, I was still a good Lutheran girl from the sticks. The subtle complexities of the human psyche and the pleasures of S&M were alien; I did not have much with which to work. Casey wanted my Miss Julie to be vulnerable, raw, and believable but he couldn't get me there.

"Lower your status," he commanded in his normal speaking voice, which was deep, resonant, and surprisingly British-sounding (he was from Nebraska). He was a serious Shakespearean actor, and no matter what words Casey uttered, they always sounded like *to-morrow and to-morrow and to-morrow creeps in this petty pace from day to day.*

I adopted a simpering lilt: "Give me orders–"

"Lower your status," he repeated.

I said the line again, now a mournful cadence.

"Oh, please." Casey was exasperated. He wanted me to elicit a real response from my acting partner. If Julie wants Jean to shrug, then fine, she should snivel despondently, but if she wants Jean to compel her to kill herself, she might demean herself to the point that he is willing to issue the self-execution order. Julie's goal suggests some aggressive tactics on her part, thus on the part of the performer.

"Give me orders," I implored in a strained voice, "and I'll obey like a dog. Do me this last service! Save my honor—"

"Like a dog," Casey reminded me.

84

I got down on all fours (that is, if knees count as feet).
"Do you will it and order me to accomplish it—"

"Lower your status."

I lay on my stomach. By enacting abasement, I started
to be abased. Here I was, in front of the whole class,
willingly responding to commands from my teacher that
seemed to *require* me to perform the next, degrading move.
I touched, then caressed, the boot of Jean. I rested my head
on same boot (gag, because it was just this dude's regular
shoe in which he walked around New York every day—the
sidewalk, the street, the subway, I smelled it all).

"Lower!"

I could not go lower than the floor, so instead, I French-
kissed the boot. *Please, Casey, please—let this lesson be over.*

I swear Jean's foot squirmed in revulsion (or maybe
he was turned on, or both). My classmates watched,
unblinking. I had foul shoe taste in my mouth, along
with some kind of schmutz, and I felt I'd failed Casey. To
my chagrin, I started to sob, or rather, I didn't prevent
myself from falling apart right there in front of everybody. I clung to Jean's pant leg for support and, without
thinking, pressed my face into his leg—real tears, real
snot—and managed to get the line out: *You know what I
ought to will, but don't will. Do you will it and order me to
accomplish it.*

And hey! I was Miss Julie. I was aware of being enormously powerful, even as I collapsed into an anguished heap. Maybe Casey and my classmates were stirred by the human wreckage before them, although probably, they were mainly thinking *Blcchh, she licked his boot.*

I learned, that day, something about playing status and actions, about aligning with the character, about playing the scene. At NSC, consequential personal and artistic revelations were frequent, therefore often experienced and observed as routine: *Ho-hum, another breakthrough.* But this lesson, for me, was exhilarating, in part because social life is, itself, a kind of performance, and to really understand status is to understand how we all operate.[20]

Then—that one night, in our East Village sublet, Greg's and mine—I was jolted from my slumber with the certainty that something baleful was upon me.

---

20 If that thought is even slightly intriguing to you, you might want to pick up a copy of Keith Johnstone's classic, *Impro.* Johnstone was the pioneer of status play in theater training, and his observations and descriptions of what motivates human behavior (which underpin most good acting and all good improvisation) exploded into public awareness with Theatresports™ and the televised improv show, *Whose Line Is It, Anyway?*

It starts with a sense of suffocation and weakness or tingling, and then your tongue feelth thwollen. The scalp crawls, the hands go numb, the inevitable approaches, and you have to DO SOMETHING OR IT WILL GET YOU. That—as maybe you already know—is a panic attack. You usually don't have just one: fearing their recurrence can induce more. They become a thing that sometimes comes over and disables you, like hiccups or migraines.

Many weeks after my wee-hours dismissal by the Beth Israel nurse, our whole class went up to the Catskills with our teachers for the month of July. The Conservatory held a summer program in Kerhonkson, not far from New Paltz. There were dormitories, a dining hall, and a big open rehearsal space, all housed in the dilapidated but serviceable buildings of a former Borscht Belt resort. The Kerhonkson campus had a timeless, humid, woodsy, grassy atmosphere that was enchanting: moss, waterfalls, tree frogs, and a comical, semi-domesticated (or rather, actor-tolerant) wild turkey that my friend Sheila and I called *Kerhonk*. The turkey's schtick was to greet arriving cars up at the turnoff, then to lead the way—wide-eyed, fluffing his wings and gobbling—fifty yards down the rutted road to the parking lot, our overexcitable, avian valet.

Every morning, actors met for a physical warm-up in the Pool Studio, a spacious, old, barnlike structure next to a swimming pool. Then breakfast, then classes until lunch. We had an afternoon break to study lines, practice skills, or swim, followed by more classes, kitchen crew duties, dinner, then rehearsals or performances. The long days concluded with everyone sitting under the stars, around a bonfire, singing, smoking, and drinking wine. I had found my tribe, my avocation, and my place. I wanted to never leave. That I might experience a second attack, especially under these joyful conditions, never occurred to me.

I was in the Pool Studio with Lilith and Betty, two friends, exploring the connection between breathing, movement, the resistance provided by the floor, and the production of glossolalia. This was a creative expansion of our regular vocal work, which was designed to improve lung capacity and strengthen the muscles of the throat and mouth. Here, we'd just taken the exercises further. Conceive, if you will, of a combination of screeching, ululating, groaning, and singing, an alingual, improvisational opera: *GnshneeCH!CH!CH!mayrjkotoooAAHH!* None of us would—*ever*—have an occasion to put this newfound talent to use (unless, I suppose, we all happened to be cast in a musical comedy version of *The Exorcist*), but you don't get to writhe on the floor in the name of experimentation, making loud, nonsensical noises—not as an adult, not in this life—without disturbing others (and getting yourself committed). Therefore, doing it is transgressive, liberating, and thrilling.

SnyagnomminolnyogliiSHHH—! All at once, I felt peculiar, out-of-body. What had happened, in all probability, was that I'd depleted my oxygen supply and made myself giddy. But a sense of doom quickly exacerbated a moment of lightheadedness to distress. I stood up and took off walking, very fast, away from the studio. Maybe I could outrun it.

Betty—just the sort of empathetic, sensible, witty person you'd want at your side as you expire from mysterious causes—followed me up and down the meadow around which the campus buildings were clustered. "Just walk with me," I shakily implored. Into the woods, down a dirt road, back to the meadow, and around the meadow again. Whatever it was, if it caught up, it would kill me, even though it was inside me. You're thinking *I recognize a histrionic personality when I see one*, but I'm not. I hate being the center of attention (which, come to think of it, does make acting an odd choice of career, but when I'm onstage—directed, rehearsed, confident, and in character—it's different: I'm not exposed, but hidden). I wasn't being melodramatic as I raced around the property. I really wanted the icky feeling to stop.

When at last we sank to the ground beneath a willow, Betty put her hand on my head, the pressure of her touch sending a sensation of pins and needles from the point of contact through my neck and shoulders, into my arms and hands, my stomach, and down my legs. I felt immobilized.

At length, when I could stand, we went to tell the program director, Albert, that I should see a physician. The nearest one was in Poughkeepsie. Someone took me there. The doctor found nothing physically wrong, gently suggesting that anxiety may have had something to do with causing or exacerbating my experience. Annoyed, I rejected this explanation. "This does not feel like anxiety!" I protested. "It feels like something really bad is about to happen to me!" He was nice enough not to direct me to a dictionary to look up the definition of anxiety.

Instead, he gave me a prescription for Xanax which, after trying it, I didn't want. Unmedicated, I had another attack a few days later. This resulted in Jimmy Tripp—a gifted teacher and a kind man, funny, bawdy, and gay— removing me from the campus for a weekend retreat at his nearby farmhouse, where I sipped mint tea in a lawn chair and, at Jimmy's suggestion, began reading his dog-eared copy of *Middlemarch*. You would be psychologically astute to suspect that I secretly longed to have Jimmy look after me, to reap the rewards of his compassion, to be set apart, and that I had therefore arranged to bring that about by falling mysteriously ill. It's a reasonable interpretation, but it's wrong. I'd had no idea that Jimmy even owned a nearby farmhouse, much less that he or anybody would offer me respite, and again, I don't much enjoy being fussed over.

At Jimmy's suggestion, I made an appointment with a therapist in a nearby village, Dr. Katz*. I'd never been to a therapist and didn't see the need, as these fits of dread and paralysis were clearly physical, not emotional—but I was up for trying anything. Our meeting was a one-off by mutual agreement, as I was going to be in Kerhonkson for only another week. There, in Dr. Katz's unassuming office, over the course of an extremely productive hour, I learned—only by hearing myself say it out loud—that I operated under the unexamined premise that I wasn't supposed to live an ordinary life. I was fortunate: healthy, sufficiently bright, loved by my parents. I'd been brought up right. I could draw and play instruments. I could read, write, and remember things, and I was supposed to use all of these endowments to make the world a better place. This I had concocted all on my own, with no pressure from anybody: I should be exceptional, but I was perpetually falling short, perpetually failing. Driving myself was how I compensated, and panic attacks were one expression of driving myself.

Dr. Katz—since she wouldn't be seeing me going forward—recommended two books to help me get a handle on the perfectionism: Claire Weekes' *Hope and Help for Your Nerves* and Karen Horney's *Neurosis and Human Growth*. I read them. But more importantly, I finished and loved *Middlemarch* (Jimmy gave me his copy) in which everyone's personality is complex yet consistent, their behavior comprehensible if not irreproachable, their failings forgivable, their relationships messy, and nobody's perfect.

Though I eventually learned to recognize and manage them—they went away altogether by the time I was in my early thirties—I would submit to occasional panic attacks for at least the next couple of years. They came over me when I had forgotten all about them; when I had begun to feel, once again, that everything was going extraordinarily well.

Chapter 7

How It Could Happen[21]

Maybe it's an accident or something dark and terrible
Maybe it's a razor blade when life becomes unbearable
It could be an aeroplane, which plummets to the ground
Or possibly a heart attack with no one else around
Maybe it's a hurricane that blows you through the air
Or a shocking current from the electric chair
What about a blazing fire that burns you to a cinder
And then you might get your head caught in a Waring
    blender
It could be an overdose, a bullet in the ear

---

21 I wrote this ditty in my early twenties, one afternoon when I was feeling glib about the seemingly limitless ways we can perish. Years later, I decided to open my play, *The House Not Touched by Death*, with it. The tune has a bouncy, kazoo-and-oompah-band feel to it. If the world is still here, if the internet is still around, and if I still have a website when this book is published, you can hear it at https://jannalgoodwin. com/how-it-could-happen/

Or maybe you'll be comatose and lie there for a year
Be careful of the toilet: you might fall in and drown
A bomb could really spoil it and leave pieces all around
It could be quite boring; it might happen in bed
One minute you'll be snoring and suddenly be
Dee-n-dee-n-dee dee dee
Just an inventory of possibility
I don't care how it happens
So long as it's not happening
To me
Not happening to me
Not to me
Nosirree, Bob
No way, no how
Uh-uh
Not me...not me...not me...

"Hey, Kath—"

"What's up?"

"—so I'm noticing that the garage door opener puts a lot of tension on the cable when it lifts the door."

"Uh-huh."

"And I'm noticing that, when I am standing in position to push the garage door opener button, I'm directly in line with that cable."

"Uh-huh."

I have known Kathy since elementary school. One year, we both took part in a week-long summer field trip program. Along with twelve other preadolescents including Kathy's younger brother, Johnny, we'd pile into a van in the morning; get hauled off to some unusual, informative, and educational destination; get the tour; goof off; redistribute the food our mothers had packed; and arrive back at the school parking lot by three p.m. I can remember visiting sand dunes, a fish farm, an open-pit uranium mine,[22] a working ranch, and a lake.

On the lake day, Kathy and Johnny sat on a dock entertaining us all with their *a cappella* version of The Diamonds' *Dear Abby*, a tuneful sendup of the advice column. The Diamonds were a ribald lounge act that the parental Corbetts had enjoyed on a trip to New York, and whose LP they'd brought home as a souvenir. The siblings had memorized the whole album, including the delivery, which they'd perfected. Stanzas culminating in wicked punch lines (*So many people write to me, you know I'd like to throttle every one of them, and go on out and get myself a bottle!* and *I suggest you find a way to keep your girlfriend on her feet!*) were belted with the gusto of Fanny Brice. It would

---

22 Wyoming, kids! Am I right?

have been wholly inappropriate had any of us, including the performers themselves, understood the references and double-entendres, but we were nine.[23] I judged the act to be hysterical and wanted to get to know these two clowns.

Neither Kathy nor I was predisposed to hair ribbons, flowery dresses, or pink, but with her short, dark curls, an endearing gap between her two front teeth, and a lanky, slightly bowlegged swashbuckle, she was even less girly than I. My dad drove her and Johnny home after one of our field trips. As they got out of the car, I called out *G'bye, Johnny! G'bye, Kathy!*

"Kathy," Dad mused unironically as we pulled away from the curb. "There's an unusual name for a boy."

Although we couldn't have known it at the time, we were in for a lifetime of friendship, and friendship sometimes means taking calls such as this one:

"If the cable were to snap—"

"The garage door would stop moving."

"—the cable would whip back and take off my head," I proposed simultaneously.

---

23 Writing this, I texted Kathy to confirm my memories of the song. I found The Diamonds' eponymous album online, sent her the link, and within the space of a few minutes, apparently both listening, we had the following exchange. Me: This is dirty. Then, after a bit, Kathy: Dear God.

"No—"

"Or lobotomize me," I added.

"You're talking about your garage door opener," Kathy reviewed, in case she'd missed something. Her tone hovered annoyingly just this side of merriment, and I also detected a hint of incredulity.

"I'm wary of it," I said.

This conversation would become—I recently learned—the basis of a one-liner with which Kathy and her wife, Bonnie, still comfort and amuse themselves. *At least*, they say, sometimes apropos of nothing, *I'm not afraid of my garage door opener.*

A cable could snap, fly back, and sever a person instantly from her life. It's not outside the realm of possibility. However, if you search the internet for *garage door opener fatalities,* you will find yourself reassured. Accounts of cable-related carnage are not abundant in the record, a bit of a letdown. I did find one or two cases in which a garage door opener or one of its components fell onto a person, which had not, up until then, been a source of concern.

Ask, however, *can a garage door kill you?* (thanks to Google's algorithms, if you're me, the question auto-fills after you've only typed *Can a ga*—) and you'll learn that yes, it can. Faulty springs, heavy doors dropping, over-confident

DIY-ers trying to fix a lift apparatus when the manual says to have it serviced by a professional—all these are causes, in one way or another, of death by garage door.

You'll probably be wanting me to check my copy of *Injury Facts*, too, so I just did. *Garage doors* and *garage door openers* did not even make it into the extensive index, but *paintball* did.

The global economy is powered by *could happens* and the agitation they provoke. What accounts for the universal, human compulsion to entertain dire contingencies?

Our developed sympathetic nervous system—which includes anxiety, fear, and the adrenaline-fueled *fight-flight-freeze* response—is not only useful; it is arguably why we're here today alongside the other present-day organisms with whom we share well-honed survival instincts. But (besides language and critical thinking) it is the human imagination that sets us apart from beasts.[24] Imagination evolved central to human survival: we can picture all kinds of unreal scenarios and prepare for them, and we can modify our actions based on envisioned

---

24 To these, philosopher Bertrand Russell would add fire, agriculture, and large-scale cooperation. Some would include property, and others would say the cerebral cortex is the distinction, at which point I've lost interest.

consequences. Because we are symbol-using animals,[25] we can also explain our misgivings to others, transmit warnings in great detail, formulate predictions, and reflect together, after the fact, about what went well and what we need to improve.

To this biological proclivity for anticipatory drama add our love of storytelling, plus the novel capacity to communicate pert-near instantaneously (if not wisely) across great distances. Add, too, mediated discourses in which *could happen* replaces the more factual, often less-gripping *is happening* and *did happen*. Amplify all that on platforms whose developers and investors build fortunes from the traffic of information, misinformation, disinformation, antipathy, and hysteria. Make easily available and normative all sorts of appealing technologies and devices, and cultivate widespread screen addiction. *Voilà!* You've got a universally overstimulated, uneasy (if not pissed-off), restless (if not jittery) global population. Among whom I feel at home, but not at ease.[26]

Books New and Old, read the sign. Godfather's occupies an unpretentious storefront on Commercial Street in

---

25 —as literary theorist Kenneth Burke has called us—
26 Sit me down with a bunch of hardcore COVID-19 conspiracy (or apocalypse) theorists, and I come off as downright insouciant.

Astoria, Oregon. It is exactly the kind of establishment that pulls us in when we're traveling. For Michael and me, strolling around unfamiliar (preferably foggy) streets, stumbling across a bookstore-café, and reading at a wobbly table while sipping a hot beverage amounts to a peak experience. Better yet if these pleasures converge near some large body of water whose shoreline we can later discover (here, we had the mighty Columbia emptying into the wide, blue Pacific) and a brewery (Astoria boasts several, but notably, the Astoria Brewing Company overlooks the river). If you also have your health, a job you don't mind, someone besides yourself to care about, and a sense of humor, there is nothing more in life to want.

We were on our way to Long Beach, in the southwestern corner of Washington, for a few days of do-nothingness at a beachfront motel I'd found online. Neither of us had ever visited the area. A devotée of the internet's array of tools, I'd had a high old time plotting our various stops, from Portland to Astoria to Long Beach and back down the coast to Seaside. The territory we would cover was limited, we had plenty of time, and it was not likely to be an eventful, much less stressful, trip.

Today, we had checked out the Astoria Column, a tower on top of a hill. There are two things I'll append to that adequate description: a) the observation deck is reached by means of an enclosed, circular staircase, and b) it is worth the claustrophobia and the effort.

Next, we'd visited the maritime museum and the Lightship Columbia (WLV-604), which was unforgettable. The vessel—a floating lighthouse, moored from 1951 until 1979 in an area known as the Graveyard of the Pacific—(!27)—had a foghorn that could be heard from five miles away and a Duplex 500mm electric lens lantern on the foremast that was visible for thrice that distance.

WLV-604 helped ships at sea to locate the entrance to the Columbia River and to navigate the hazardous crossing of sandbars at the river's mouth. The lightship had a permanent, eighteen-man crew furnished with everything they needed to live out there for long tours—weeks—since crappy weather and rough seas often made it hard to deliver supplies.

You wouldn't think that this, of all fantasies, would appeal to me—to *me*—but it did. It does. In a brief documentary we watched before boarding, the captain recalled sobbing sailors, ready to dive off the boat out of desperation—but I feel I may have been able to tough out the hardships. Even if I'd been made of the right stuff, as a

---

27 Since 1792, over *two thousand ships and seven hundred lives* have been lost in this area, which one source refers to as a "navigational nightmare."

woman I would not have been eligible for the crew back then. So when I picture me out there toiling, braving the elements, being violently buffeted by currents, tides, and swells, suffering the tedium, enduring the close-up foibles and fragrances of others, and saving lives, rather than getting into a snit about how I would have had to disguise myself (binding my breasts, hiding my period) and fake masculine traits (belching, speaking gruffly, scratching my crotch, biting off the heads of lizards) I instead just see myself as a strong, young man, one whose temperament would have been less circumspect and far more matey than Janna's. My name would have been Will.

After the lightship, Michael and I had meandered down Commercial Street looking for warmth and caffeine. We'd found both, and books, at Godfather's, and here we were, waiting for two espressos while perusing the shelves. The cover of Bonnie Henderson's *The Next Tsunami* caught my eye and I pulled it down for a closer look. *Living on a Restless Coast*, the subtitle further explicated. Well, that's compelling, I thought. I would enjoy reading about Japan or Indonesia while reclining on the patio outside our room in Long Beach, listening to the waves rolling in. A disaster enthusiast, I found the *could happen* inveiglement effective. Plus, who wouldn't want to become more familiar with the geological mechanisms—not to mention the psychological, social, political, economic, and scientific interpretations, the experiences, and the costs—of these sudden, awe-inspiring displacements of large volumes of water?

An editorial blurb on the flap began well but ended badly: *Watching the horrific devastation of tsunamis in Southeast Asia, Chile, and Japan, it is easy to forget that the same outcome is possible along the coast of America's Pacific Northwest. Henderson redresses this omission, focusing on Oregon's swath of the Ring of Fire, that Pacific belt responsible for 90% of the world's earthquakes.*

I flipped past the table of contents only to land on a map of the northwestern Oregon/southwestern Washington coastal region. A cutout brought into sharper focus a section of this map, framing a peninsula. The community of Long Beach was on it, a sitting duck. Had I been able to enlarge the cutout even more—I tried expanding my fingers over its surface, but the page must have been broken—I would have seen featured, at the center of the danger zone, the roof of the motel where I'd made our reservations for the next three nights.

You can bet that I purchased that book. If it hadn't been for sale, I'd have stolen it.

Let me see if I—a non-geologist with no more than a passing, literary acquaintance with how the planet is assembled—can explain subduction. If you're already cognizant, feel free to follow along with a critical attitude (jot down and save your comments for our next Zoom happy hour) and if you're not, go ahead and take my lecture seriously, but with a small grain of what geologists know as sodium chloride.

I suppose we'd first want to recall that the Earth's mantle—a molten layer of silicate rock eighteen hundred or so miles thick—churns due to convection, which is the process by which heated material, magma, rises to become new crust while older, denser, cooler material is sucked downwards. As this new crust forms in the depths of the ocean, it spreads or diverges from its origins. You might think of a loaf of the round, French bread known as a *boule*, and how it splits when baking, the gooey dough inside rising to push the browning cracks wider. Whether or not this is a legitimate analogy, it makes sense to me, a bread lover, and even if I have it wrong, hey, you got to think about a nice, fat, crusty loaf of French bread for a second. Tectonic plates are massive slabs of solid rock, created through the process described above, that can be anywhere from a few hundred miles to thousands of miles across. These slabs are made up of oceanic and continental lithosphere—the platy layer of the Earth's shell—and drift around on the more viscous asthenosphere, moving at the rate of an inch or two per year.

Some continental plates pull apart (East Africa's Rift Zone). Some drift horizontally past each other (the San Andreas fault). Some collide and cause the crumpling upwards that we call mountains (think the Himalayas, still rising). Beneath the ocean, some plates thrust under others, which can cause a different kind of upheaval— hotspots and volcanos, cracks, faults, quakes. A subduction zone is where one plate is moving beneath another, to be reabsorbed by the molten material below.

The Juan de Fuca Plate is produced by the oceanic spreading center known as the Juan de Fuca Ridge, and it is subducting just about fifty miles off the coast from British Columbia all the way to Northern California: the zone is six hundred and eighty miles long. *Who is this Juan de Fuca*, you may wonder aloud, mispronouncing his name as you do.

Ioannis Phokas was a sixteenth-century Greek explorer, probably the first European to land on the North American west coast. He sailed under the Spanish flag. His crew obviously gave up on getting his name right, and out of all the alternatives proposed one riotous night over a cask of brandy (*Juan, Cap'n Moussaka, Whatever,* and *Ph**kus*), in spite of way more votes for the latter, it was *Juan* that stuck.

The tectonic plate named in his honor is a remnant of the once ginormous (even by tectonic plate standards)

Farallon Plate, which has been drawn beneath the North American Plate. The convergence of the two plates is known as the Cascadia Subduction Zone.

If you are interested in the edifying if not unputdown-able—I found it to be both—story of how scientists figured all this out, you will want to read Henderson's book, or any other number of excellent works on the subject. For now, let's move on to the larger point: *YOU HAVE GOT TO BE KIDDING ME*. To that end, while these do not necessarily reflect the intended thesis, here is a summary of my personal takeaways:

1. Science is the greatest survival tool humans have ever developed, and while all scientists are cool, Earth scientists get to go to the bottom of the ocean in a submersible.

2. Good science is like solving a puzzle, but first you have to identify what the puzzle is, what parts belong to it, and what parts do not—and then, you get to go to the bottom of the ocean in a submersible.

3. I wouldn't personally want to do that, but I admire those who do.

4. The Juan de Fuca Plate seems to be *caught* on the North American Plate as it subducts. Pressure has built up and continues to build. One day, like a garage

door cable snapping, something will give; pressure will release, and this event will send a lot of water toward the coast—

5. —a LOT of water—
6. —to and over the Long Beach peninsula, and
7. There is no way to accurately predict when this will happen.

When it does, though (and, because strong evidence has been uncovered indicating past, periodic oceanic quakes and tsunamis in the region, the thinking goes that it certainly will), there won't be much warning. Communities up and down the coast and inland will be washed away; others, substantially shaken. Seattle's waterfront may be— get this—liquefied. *Liquefaction* means that the vibrations caused by the quake result in solid ground behaving like quicksand: highways and structures sink into it. Olympia, Tacoma, Portland, Eugene, and Salem will all be wrecked. This "Big One" could/would/will be far more devastating than anything the infamous San Andreas—a mere "strike-slip" fault, where plates slide past one another—might serve up.

Traveling to Long Beach from Astoria, you first pass a headland called Cape Disappointment, where explorers before Louis and Clark once looked for and found the mouth of the Columbia but mistook it for just another stupid bay. *Aww*, they tweeted before leaving to continue their search, *Just another stupid bay! #Disappointed.* Coming down onto the peninsula, you pass signs depicting a person running from a giant wave. *Tsunami Hazard Zone*, the signs warn, and *Tsunami Evacuation Route.* When you enter the town proper, frantically scanning for elevation, you note that there is none. Everything is flat, flat, flat. It is hard to see how this place isn't already underwater. Your motel is on a flat stretch of flat land leading to the very long, very wide, flat beach. The motel clerk, the housekeepers pushing carts between buildings, the kids on skateboards in the parking lot all strike you as oblivious. Several girls on horses gallop between you and the breakers, shouting gleefully, unaware of what is about to happen.

A boardwalk and trail run for miles through the dunes. After you've unpacked your bags, you saunter along it at a restrained pace meant to suggest—mainly to yourself— that you are a carefree person, one hundred percent free of care. You have dinner at a restaurant that you chose for its second-floor deck, from which you can keep a close eye on the water as you eat. In the room, you are mindful of tremors. Lying in bed next to your husband, you devour as much of *The Next Tsunami* as you can handle, dropping off during a relatively safe part of the narrative, when the scientists are at a conference at the University of Washington, discussing their findings.

I finished the book the next morning before we'd even had our coffee. Then, as we poked around the peninsula, I mentally designed things that might be climbed onto in case of a tsunami. One of these ideas resembled the Space Needle. I knew it would be an addition to Long Beach's low skyline that everyone, locals and visitors alike, would appreciate when the time came. There would be an elevator inside and circular stairs around the outside (so more people could get up to the top rapidly in a tidal wave event). The large disc at the top would hold one hundred occupants (arbitrary, but easy to remember). The structure could be benignly designated a—a *highpoint*, for example. Highpoints would have to be built at reasonable intervals up and down the peninsula.

As much as I enjoyed the notion of being secure in a highpoint when the ocean came rushing ashore, I could not help but think of the unfortunates—the elderly, the disabled, little kids—who wouldn't make it in time. For them, I imagined sturdy, waterproof "bubbles" that could be left scattered all over the place. Each bubble would seat up to eight adults (you'd strap in as you do on a carnival ride) and, while these would not be as good as highpoints, you could get inside and at least they'd float. Starting with the problem of how to provide stabilization and oxygen to the bubble, I spent the next several hours ruminating on materials, construction, maintenance, durability, safety, and costs. By the end of the day I had a headache, and there was still no place Michael and I could run to if Cascadia were to pop that night.

For much of my life, I've found peace and joy, whenever I needed it, in a small, two-story cottage on a cliff overlooking a cove. The cottage is embraced, in the front, by a squat hedge that parts to admit a brick path from the road, up one step, past flowerpots, to the door. Downstairs, a cozy kitchen hunkers around a stone fireplace. Pots and pans hang from an iron railing above the gas stove, cooking utensils from hooks on the stove's side. The surface of the walls is uneven, imperfect. The ceilings are beamed, the stairs dark wood, polished by time and use. There is a sitting room, a library, and a WC on the ground floor, which opens in the back to a veranda. Upstairs are two bedrooms, a bath, and a study with a sun porch from which I can look out to sea. On the sun porch sit two comfy armchairs and a loveseat of rattan with worn cushions, a couple of small tables for my tea and cookies, and an Amish Mission-style chair at a table that can be used as a desk. Out back, a garden of yellow roses borders a short, level lawn shaded by two mature evergreens. The lawn gives over to a bluff that ends at the beach below. A wooden staircase of no more than twenty steps leads down to it. Some days, the cottage is wrapped in a thick fog and only the sounds of the waves tell me where I am. Other days are stormy, with high winds and beating rain, even snow. In the evening, the sun does not glare; the lay of the land and the trees block direct light after late afternoon. This cottage is in Cornwall. Or it is north of Mendocino. Or in France, or Iceland. It has also been near Puerto Vallarta. A few times, it was in Maine. It is always near a village, where I can have breakfast or get a cup of strong coffee, buy groceries, see a film (an old film, black and white) and have a pint with friends. There are two Mexican restaurants in the village: the one I like, and the one I never go to.

Nothing bad ever happens at the cottage which, by the way, has superb Wi-Fi. I live there, I take care of the property, I write, and I make dinner for me and Michael, or he cooks. On occasion, we have a dog, a patchy mongrel, but I do not want to waste my daydream taking him for a walk or remembering to feed him, so I more frequently leave him out. Because I am selfish.

———

Our last day in Long Beach, we hiked around Ledbetter State Park, which is—we found out when in the middle of it—a low-lying area prone to tidal flooding, so the experience had that going for it. That night, I lay awake with my eyes closed, letting my cottage come to me. It is elusive; I can't just conjure it up. When it finally appeared, I had to initiate exigency measures for the first time ever. I could see that it wasn't high enough above sea level. And its proximity to the edge of the bluff was suddenly problematic: a landslide, quake, or liquefaction could cause the whole shebang to collapse. I reviewed the underpinnings, realizing that I'd need to bolt the cottage to the rock beneath with steel beams in order to feel secure this close to where the pounding waves were causing erosion. Too near the sea, I would always feel vulnerable. Too far, and what was the point, since I wanted to hear the surf? For much of the night, I revised, rebuilt, and re-situated until my original Happy Place was in shambles, and I didn't have a substitute.

Thus began my search for a new Happy Place, which was more taxing than you might suppose. With climate change, woodsy lakefront cabins are increasingly jeopardized by forest fires, forget about the likelihood of hooligan break-ins during weeks when I might forget to pretend to be there. The Pacific Northwest will always have Cascadia; the coast of California, San Andreas. Galveston and anywhere southeast, on the Gulf? Get out of here! The waves aren't crashy enough, the houses are on stilts—not for no reason—and mosquitoes abound. Mentally, I traversed the globe, finding only problems and threats: global warming and sea level rise, geological hotspots and earthquake proneness, flooding, desert-like heat, giant hornets, gamma rays, you name it. Just before sunrise, I devised a spaceship, my own personal one, connected to others by some kind of reliable network. All of us—humanity—might fly up and live in little, self-contained worlds.[28] But, a retreat to space felt too drastic to be comforting. No, I had to find another way to fall asleep, even for a couple of hours, because it was going to be a long day. Michael and I had a drive ahead of us—not far to Seaside, but then back to Portland—followed by a plane trip home to Colorado.

And then, I remembered WLV-604. Below deck, adjacent to the galley with its solidly-anchored dinettes and cabinets, I'd seen berths, sturdy bunks stacked one-on-one,

---

28 Little did I know that, not too far in the future, the novel coronavirus would force us all into a situation rather like this. It would turn out to be weird and lonely, and even a recluse like myself would long for face-to-face, normal human contact and the pleasures of sitting around a table, talking, eating, and watching each other smile.

where worn-out seamen had once rested their weary heads
in between long, grueling shifts. I had lingered in those
quarters, feeling like I wanted to lie down, knowing that,
after a long day of hard and noble labor, I could doze off
there and dream, held firm by the metal frame and railings,
tucked into the side of the Lightship Columbia's solid hull,
rocked to slumber even as she was tossed about on dark,
troubled waters.

Thinking about it, I conked out within minutes and
slept for a long time, the launch of my new—and still reliable today—Happy Place.

Come to find out, I'm not the only one to have been obsess-
ing about ways to ride out the inevitable tsunami that will
hit Long Beach. A Seattle-based engineering company
came up with what has been referred to as an "evacuation
berm," a "mini-mountain," and (my favorite) a "tsunami
safe haven." This is a man-made hill, its ocean-facing edge
shaped like the prow of a ship to help deflect the force
of the incoming wave. You run up it and stay there until
the danger has come and gone. It holds eight hundred,
so it is for sure an improvement upon the highpoint. The
citizens of Long Beach are supportive, and so am I, as I've
barely stopped thinking about their problem since our trip,
which was a few years ago.

And the bubble? One now exists: the Survival Capsule.[29] An aeronautical engineer on vacation with his family in Cannon Beach, Oregon, "envisioned a personalized safety system against the threat of a tsunami," according to the company's website, and he invented the very thing I already invented. Since he actually designed, engineered, and built it, while I just thought about it and drew but a single blueprint (on a napkin, while at Custard King) I have no claim on the intellectual property and do not intend to pursue any kind of legal action. But so you know I'm not lying:

Honestly, I'm just glad it got made.

---

29 The first person in the United States to purchase a Survival Capsule was Jeanne Johnson, a resident of Ocean Park on the Long Beach peninsula.

Chapter 8

The Almighty

I told you earlier, I talk to God on occasion. I have no evidence that our relationship is reciprocal, but to the extent I have been able to ascertain—using the exact same methods we all use, namely, self-serving fabrication—I can report that having a part about Him was His idea. It is not easy to make out the will of God, but I'm pretty sure what He said to me was, "Gina, just wanted you to know that I would be willing to collaborate, to make sure the part about Me in your book is awesome."

"Janna," I corrected Him. "It's Janna."

"No, about Me."

"You are not really featured," I said, gently but firmly. "It's more about the naturally-arising fears, and the learned and cultivated ones, that sometimes serve to protect us and ensure our survival, but which can also undermine our own health and the health of society. It's about how we reproduce patterns of anxiety that can come to feel—"

"We." He rolled it around in His Mouth like a marble.

"Okay, not You. People. We're pretty good at identifying and responding to threats posed by the elements, but we often ignore, misconstrue, and underesti—"

"Jesus H. Christ," He muttered. I would inquire later as to whether H. is, in fact, Jesus' middle initial, and if so, what it stands for. "Wake Me when you get to Me."

"You can't give me thirty seconds of Your time to finish a thought?"

"When you go on and on, I stop caring."

"You stop caring because You're checking Facebook."

"I am not."

"I can see that You are. And by the way, the research on devices and social interaction clearly demonstrates that You can't do that and this at the same time." I am a trained Professor of Communication, which ought to count for something in a conversation about conversation. "It's called *phubbing*. You're not present; You're not really here."

That, incidentally, is the whole wrong thing to say to God. But it didn't matter. He wasn't paying attention. He was now watching a YouTube video of goats that sound exactly like human beings, crying out in anguish and fear. *AAANGHHH!* Which is a riot, and makes God laugh really hard.

AAANGHHH! From my days at Kerhonkson, I know how good—necessary, even—it feels to bleat plaintively without rhyme, reason, or restraint. Even so, one afternoon, when that sort of thing had gone on (for hours) in the alley right outside my study, I called the cops on Oscar. You remember Oscar, our homeless-not-homeless neighbor?

"I don't want to get this guy in trouble—" I began, and explained the situation.

Dispatcher wanted to know, "Has the individual ever threatened or harmed you?"

"No, not precisely."

She sighed, saying she'd send an officer over. I watched from an upstairs window. Eventually, a squad car pulled up. A kind-faced policewoman got out. She had a few words with Oscar, who piled up his belongings without complaint, tossing armloads in the dumpster. Off he went down the alley, empty-handed. *Wow,* I thought. *That was easy. Bada-bing.*

That night, Michael and I were awakened by a big "BADA-BOOM!" It sounded like a dumpster bursting into flames, and when we looked outside, guess what? Fire trucks, sirens, lights, hubbub…and in the morning, the once-proud, stiff plastic upper lip of the dumpster lid had melted into snarly fangs over a blackened maw. Oscar could not have sculpted it to appear more hostile.

A few days later here he was again, more belligerent than ever, claiming an even bigger circumference. This time, cleverly, we did NOT call the police. We'd gotten the message, and didn't want our house to go up in smoke. I'm not saying Oscar would do that, and I'm not saying he wouldn't.

He's still out there. Once or twice a week, he goes on a tirade. Beats up his cart, smacks the dumpster, strides up and down the alley shouting, "BRING IT ON! YOU LAME-ASS, PISSANT DOUCHEBAG! COME AND GET SOME A ME! AAANGHHH!"

The day Michael and I got home from the Grand Canyon (the trip that inspired my solo writing retreat in Wyoming, hence the present stew of stories) I was out in the driveway, hauling in our suitcases, and we came face-to-face, Oscar and I. We made eye contact at what would have been striking distance had either of us been a snake.

I wasn't prepared for an encounter. My guard was down. I blurted out the first thing that suggested itself: "Hello!"

"Hello," Oscar said.

That night, before I went to bed, I checked on him. Turned off the lights in my study, peeked out. There he was, sitting with his back against the fence, holding a penlight over the pages of a big, hardbound book, reading. I tried but was unable to make out the title. *Dianetics? How to Train Your Dragon?* I want to know! If it is *Middlemarch*, for example, then, next time we run into each other, I can be all like, *Hey, how about that Dorothea Brooke and all her socialist ideas for housing the poor?*

I watched him down there for a long time. He didn't look up and see me. That's okay. I didn't really want him to.

Chapter 9

The Wolf and Me

When Little Red Cap entered the woods a wolf came up to her. She did not know what a wicked animal he was, and was not afraid of him.

"Good day to you, Little Red Cap."

"Thank you, wolf."

—Jacob and Wilhelm Grimm

When I was in the fifth grade, I was friends (*ish*)—briefly— with Debbie Wiegler*.

You've never heard of Debbie, but if you had been a fifth grader at Grant Elementary then, you'd have known all about her. She was one of those sturdy, self-confident, flaxen-haired girls with the loud, raspy voices who say mean things about everybody. The rest of us have to either openly admire the facility with which such girls express their aggression, or become unwitting objects of their formidable contempt. I walked a dishonest line between those two options: I feigned respect, and was therefore allowed into Debbie's circle for a few short weeks. Her conduct went against everything I'd ever been taught in Sunday School about how to treat other people, and everything I believed, but she was popular, she owned lots of Barbies, and she had a horse.

One Sunday afternoon after church, I was invited to accompany Debbie and her family up to their winter recreational base, a one-room cabin on Casper Mountain. There, her older cousin, Kevin*—who was compelling, what with the long lashes, the crooked front tooth, and the musky, unwashed tang of boy teenager—took us, Debbie first, then me, on our own, separate, individualized Skidoo rides. I had not planned for this (I figured we were coming up here to throw a few snowballs and sit in front of a fire, sipping hot chocolate) and had failed to bring a snowsuit. My gloves were made of knit cotton, and I had no hat. The Wieglers provided me with mittens and, at the last minute, Mr. Wiegler made me wear his red hunting cap, pulling the flaps down over my ears.

"Don't let the wolves get you!" Debbie's uncle called out as his son and I started out the gate for my turn. I had not considered the possibility of wolves before that moment, but even as it crossed my mind to worry, I also dismissed the thought, so as to be able to enjoy myself. *There's no wolves on Casper Mountain*, went my reasoning.

We quickly left the road, then departed from the established trail to gallivant about the white, wild, forest. When I thought we were going in one direction, we would instead go in another. I was anxious that we might get lost. What could I do but hang on? I have since come to appreciate the circumbendibus; it has gotten me where I am today, which happens to be here.

My ride would turn out to be longer than Debbie's by approximately five minutes. This was not due to a navigational error, but because we would stop in the woods so that—wrong! Good guess, but no: *not* so that Kevin could molest me. No, unpleasant sexual encounters wouldn't start happening for another few years.

For example, in high school, I would work part-time at a radio station where one night, a popular DJ—Al Smarmy*—would ask me to reach above my head to get an LP from the top shelf. While my arms were raised, my hands holding a precariously balanced stack of records, he would press against me with what I would take to be his jabby belt buckle. When he panted, grabbing my hips, heat emanating from his groin against my posterior, I would realize something gross was happening—but I would still be, essentially, a kid, in an era when girls my age from families like mine had only the vaguest of notions regarding urges and pleasure, much less assault. I would have had no acquaintance with hard-ons or sexual misbehavior. The frotteur was an adult, a local celebrity who was thought to be a decent guy. I would assume that his concupiscence was my fault. Diffidently, I would smile because politeness was programmed into my cultural if not biological DNA. I would wriggle away, blushing. I would regard the affront as creepy and upsetting and keep it to myself, pretending it had not happened. What would I say? To whom would I say it? Al would, afterwards, start openly teasing me with innuendoes, in response to which I would accommodatingly nod and giggle in spite of myself. Sometimes, our learned performances of cheerful compliance are so embedded in our moral and physical repertoire that it is a challenge to overcome their instruction.

Sitting behind him, I clung to Cousin Kevin's torso as he sped, bumped, wove, dodged, and twisted through the trees, showing off. The hunting cap kept slipping over my eyes, so much of what I remember is darkness, and the racket made by the machine. We tried conversation—mostly him yelling over his shoulder, asking if I was okay, and me yelling in his ear *WOO-OOH!* A half mile from the cabin, we might have been in the taiga of Siberia, so reduced was the population: two. Kevin slowed and cut the engine, but not, as I emphasized earlier, to take advantage of my youth, naivete, and vulnerability for his own sexual pleasure. Yes, sure, that sort of thing would happen, plenty. Not at that moment, and not at the hands of Kevin—

—but later. During my freshman year at Boston College, I was flying back to Massachusetts from Wyoming after Christmas break, and had to change planes in Minneapolis. While re-checking my guitar at the counter, fiddling with its strings to loosen them, I happened to look up at the passenger standing next to me at the counter, and knew at once I'd seen his image on television and in magazines. With him was an understated security detail, a bruiser in a dark suit with a stick up his butt. The VIP reeked of charisma; it emanated from him like Polo Green. *That's either Walter Mondale or Henry Kissinger*, I thought to myself, proud to have recognized an iconic, middle-aged man who had something to do with being in the news. We struck up a conversation, me and this personage, who it turned out was neither of the people I'd surmised. He was, however, famous. I'll call him Shmed Shmenedy.

Once I learned who he actually was—neither the Vice President nor Secretary of State, both of which I guessed aloud before he corrected me—it was neither his renowned family nor his own congressional accomplishments that sprang to mind, but rather tragedy and scandal: one night, leaving a party, he'd notoriously driven a young woman off a bridge and to her death at the bottom of a pond, had extricated and saved himself, left the scene, and had failed to report the fatal accident to the authorities. This made me not vigilant as, in retrospect, it should have, but curious.

When I told Shmed I was from Wyoming, he asked if I knew his friend, Governor Herschler. I did not. However, because like everyone else in Wyoming I knew who Herschler was, I lied a bit and said yes, I sure did. This provided the occasion to talk about Wyoming state politics, unfortunately, as I had no interest in Wyoming state politics. With an exchange of courtesies, we separated only to run into each other again, half an hour later, at the gate, where he asked if I wanted to sit with him in First Class. I felt this was a warm acknowledgment of my inoffensive personality if not my intelligence, and accepted the invitation.

First Class was everything it is cracked up to be, by the way, especially if you're not paying for it. Shmed and I chatted for a couple of hours. He was on his way home after attending Hubert Humphrey's funeral. He was still recovering from a recent trip to China. He reached into his portfolio, pulling out a People Magazine to show me a photo of himself in—yes—China. Shmed grasped and squeezed my hand as the plane landed. I let him. I supposed he was being paternal, plus, he had admitted that— like me—he found landing to be scary, if an adrenaline rush, and I wanted to reassure him. On the ground at Logan Airport, he invited me to an event at Anthony's Pier 4—a swanky place I knew by reputation only—and to an afterparty at his residence, all to take place in a few days. Thrilled, I accepted. In parting, I called him Mr. Shmenedy. *Call me Shmed*, he grinned. What big teeth he had.

I was a middle-class, asexual (my longings were bohemian, not libidinous), androgynous girl from a high plains oil town. My hair styled in a spiky, Rod Stewart shag, I walked with what I thought was a roguish swagger and stood with my weight on one leg, hip cocked. I was not sophisticated. Nothing so far—except, perhaps, my parents' insistence on *please, thank you,* and proper table etiquette—had prepared me to hobnob with the elite of the East Coast.

Because I owned only three K-Mart tops, a skirt, a sweater, flared Lees with holes in the knees, and a pair of clogs, my roommate and other dormies (once I'd convinced them that I wasn't making this whole thing up) helped me to prepare, just like the singing woodland creatures getting Cinderella gussied up for the ball. From their own closets, they came up with a proper dress, a good coat—not meant for winter, but snazzy—and extremely painful high heels unsuitable for walking, not to mention in January on cobblestones. I borrowed T fare, and away I tottered.

The Anthony's Pier 4 shindig was probably a political fundraiser, but what did I know of such things? The featured event was Shmed himself, narrating a slideshow of his trip while I sat among seventy other listeners, surreptitiously freeing my blistered toes from the cruel shoes for a break, then squeezing them in again.

Afterwards, a youngish man found me in the milling crowd. He introduced himself as Rick, Shmed's personal assistant. He was to bring me over to the senator's apartment. He called a car to take us to an address in Back Bay. After escorting me to the penthouse and letting me in, Rick assured me his boss would be showing up any minute. Then, he left. Abandoned, I stared out the window at the lights of Cambridge, across the river. I slipped a personalized book of matches—embossed with Shmed's wife's name (maybe I'd get to meet her, too!)—into my pocket. Then, I felt guilty, so I put the matchbook back. Then, realizing this might be the most interesting evening

I'd ever have, and wanting a small memento, I took the matchbook again, resolving to let Shmed and his wife know what I'd done and to ask them if it was okay.

When Shmed walked in, I expected him to be followed by a noisy, adoring crowd but he was alone. People would probably be showing up in a bit, he explained, preparing me a frozen daiquiri (*I love these*, he pronounced, though he wasn't drinking one himself). We sat in a conversational configuration, I on the pillowy divan, he in an armchair. I complained that my feet hurt, and he told me to kick off the shoes. To demonstrate how informal they were in the Shmenedy household, he kicked his off. Not wanting to seem uptight, I followed suit. Shmed regaled me with amusing stories about himself. I made quips and was glad when he laughed. I felt fascinating. No part of me, however, felt sexy, and at no point did I imagine physical intimacy with this married person who was exactly my father's age. That this was his intent would have struck me as ludicrous, had you entered the room right then and whispered said information in my good ear. *Bah*, I might have replied.

Eventually, Shmed admitted that no one else was coming. I was let down. As I stood to leave, he leaned in, cornering me onto the cushions. He swiftly drew his hand under my nose and cracked something open, a little ampoule. "Take a sniff!" he encouraged in a husky, insistent tone. I did, at which my head blew off my body and into the air, and I went, *WOO-OOH!*—the same sound, you might recall, that I'd made seven years earlier, while riding on the back of Kevin's snowmobile; the sensations were not dissimilar. Shmed took his own sniff, and both of us sat there, stunned expressions on our faces, for who knows how long.

What I remember of the rest of the evening was being guided woozily into one of the bedrooms, where on the wall was a very large photograph (or painting, or possibly a wall hanging) depicting Shmed and his well-known brothers on a sailboat, grinning. I remember that he was way heavier than me—that I couldn't breathe under the weight of him—and that, after he'd tried, for a long time, to gain excruciating access to my startled and resistant interior parts (in my drunken, druggy fog, I was embarrassed that Shmed couldn't do what he wanted to do, and mumbled apologies), he gave up. He rolled over, led me to a different bedroom, more or less tucked me in, and left me there until morning. When I told this story decades later, to my husband, he cracked that this must be the creed that allows Shmenedy men to hold their heads up: if you're raping a woman and she regains consciousness enough to protest, you act like a gentleman and stop.

The sun streaming in woke me. I washed up, then wandered out to the vast living room, wearing a sumptuous robe I'd found in the room. Shmed had fresh-squeezed orange juice ready for me on a tray. After I dressed, he called me a cab and gave me enough money to pay for it. While he didn't escort me down to the front door, he did watch me get into the elevator, where I stuck my hand into the closing door and delivered my exit line.

"I took a book of matches," I said, wanting to end this with a clear conscience.

"What? Oh, that's—you're welcome to them." He said goodbye and that he'd be calling me—I'd provided the extension of my dorm in Newton. He did call, twice. Once, to tell me that he'd be appearing on an interview show and to ask if I wanted to watch it (I did). The second and last time, he claimed he was calling to say hi. Both calls I took while standing in my PJs, out in the hall, on the floor's only phone.

I dropped out of college—not in the slightest having to do with Shmed, which experience was no more than a blip on a far bigger, more interesting screen—but because I wasn't ready to be there. My mind was on theater, music, the arts, entertainment, and travel. By my early twenties, I lived in West Hollywood. One December evening, as I hurried down Santa Monica Boulevard to catch a bus to my improv class, a tall, male prostitute—back then, and on that street, you knew—maneuvered me right off the sidewalk, pushing me up against a chain link fence. He held a knife near my face but didn't seem intent upon using it except to scare me into giving him my money—three dollars and fifteen cents—after which extraction he forced a tonguey kiss on me (think of someone shoving a live, squirming eel into your mouth) and grabbed my unassuming, firmly bra-encased breasts with his large, grubby hands.

Somehow, I managed to introduce myself, and also asked his name in an attempt to humanize both of us. *Dominic*, he mumbled. I took the opening: hoping to transform him from predator to protector, I wondered aloud if he might come with me to the bus stop. I didn't like to be alone on the street at night, I explained, because you never knew whom you might encounter. He blinked, considering my unusual request, then walked me to the bus, waited until I got on, and waved goodbye. I don't assume that my tactic would work on most occasions or with most assailants, but miraculously, it worked that once.

After, I would run into him again and again. I had to pass through his territory to get almost anywhere I wanted to be. *Hi Dominic!* I would merrily cry out as if we'd met doing some wholesome activity like—I don't know, square dancing—and I was pleased to see him. Times he appeared hungover or high, I'd hand him some change or offer to buy him a Martinelli's sparking apple juice from the corner market. Martinelli's sparkling apple juice was the nicest present I could afford to give somebody with whom I wished to stay on good terms so he wouldn't jump me again.

Anyhoo, back to Kevin. That is, right after this other one, which happened mere weeks after the Dominic episode. In an office directly across the street from the grand entrance to Grauman's Chinese Theater—where the view from my window of concretized handprints and sidewalk stars made it easy to fantasize about being discovered—I worked for a rare coin company, fulfilling phone orders for collectors. One day in the break room, bored, perusing the weeklies for a one-way ticket out of my cubicle, I came across a classified ad placed by a stage magician, one Eddie Cadabra*. He was looking for a *Pretty Assistant, 18-22* to gild his act. It would pay well—$50 per show. While no bombshell, I figured I was maybe pretty enough to answer the ad.

On the phone, he insisted that home auditions were quick, easy, and practical, so of course, I gave him my address. When proposing a suitable time, I added helpfully, "My housemates won't be around. They'll all be at work, so we won't be disturbed." I was living in a classic,

1930s bungalow on Norton Ave with a group of similarly starry-eyed hopefuls—David the Screenwriter, David the Musician, and Sylvia the Photographer (I was Janna the Banana, which, come to think of it, seems unfair). As promised, none were home when Mr. Cadabra, a marginally-unkempt if not quite greasy man in his forties, showed up. In our dingy, stucco living room with its hippie floor cushions and nonworking electric fireplace, he unpacked his little black bag and held out a red sequined outfit.

"This will have to fit," he told me (a premise I unquestioningly accepted, because who could afford to buy spangly costumes willy-nilly for every new assistant?). "So try it on, and then we'll go over what the assistant does during the show." I changed in the bathroom, emerging uncomfortable, but still game. The suit, a bit gappy in the chest area, made me feel like a sex object, which I hated, but now I wanted the gig, if only to prove to myself that I could nail an audition.

Mr. Cadabra wanted to know if I was claustrophobic (because for a certain illusion, I would be inside a closed container being sawed in half, and freaking out is one important thing a stage magician's assistant must not do). No, I assured him, I was not. I was, in fact, claustrophobic, but hoped this would not become an actual issue. He proposed that he try on my wrists a pair of handcuffs he'd brought, by way of easing me into the nature and feel of the job. *Why not?* I agreed. Convinced now that I had talent, he took it to the next level: I would also need to be cool with wearing a gag and a hood. "Audiences," he assured me, "love this bit."

You're thinking *You did not let him do that*, but Dear Reader, I did, and *Presto!* I was lying on the floor, my hands cuffed behind me and bound to my feet, unable to see. With a mouthful of drool-soaked bandana, I was struggling to make a verbal request—"Ish agh eye cafoofen ng?"[30] —when David the Screenwriter came in the front door, home early. David put an immediate stop to the audition, kicking the prestidigitator and his props to the curb with a promise to call the police. He immediately noted, for my edification, that even by Hollywood standards, *that* had been weird to walk in on.

So it would not be unreasonable to think that an eleven-year-old girl alone in an isolated clearing with a young man, far from prying eyes, might be—along with the man himself—vulnerable to his worst impulses. However, I assure you one last time: upon this particular occasion I was left undisturbed, those other, different experiences

---

30 "This is too tight; could you loosen it?"

waiting for me in my future. We had stopped only so that Kevin could sneak a cigarette before coming back under parental supervision. He pulled out a smashed pack of Marlboros, tapped one forth, expertly flipped open his silver lighter, thumbed the flint wheel to spark a flame, lit up, and dreamily we sat together in perfect stillness save for the snap of an occasional falling pinecone, the call of a chickadee and, when Kevin inhaled, the sizzle of burning tobacco.

"Are there really wolves?" I asked at length, because if there were, they would come when you were least expecting it, like now. He shrugged. When my teeth started to chatter from the cold, Kevin tossed away his cigarette and we started back. Nothing to see here.

But it mattered after all because, when we got to the cabin, laughing together and sharing tea from Kevin's thermos, Debbie, taking in our bonhomie, stopped speaking to me. This continued for the next hour and for the duration of the ride down the mountain. In those days, there were no headphones or cell phones involved in the Silent Treatment. A person sitting next to you in the back seat of a car could not passive-aggressively punish you by faking total immersion in her TikTok feed while you sat there hoping for normal relations to resume. Instead, she denied you eye contact and stared off into the distance.

Even in that low-tech way, you were effectively made to not exist.

Something was wrong, very wrong. But Debbie wasn't going to tell me what.

The next day, after more Not Speaking, Debbie followed me home after school with another girl, Belinda*, whom I did not like. Debbie knew I did not like Belinda. We had, up until very recently, not liked Belinda together.[31]

I think back on this as *The Day I Got Beat Up in a Field*, but to be truthful, that is not what went down. Here's what did. Debbie and Belinda walked at my heels, hand in hand, for several blocks, whispering and making snide observations about my hair, my clothes, the way I walked—I'm not sure, because I was and am (as previously noted) completely deaf on the one side. I couldn't make out what they were saying, and it's awkward to turn around and ask people to please repeat their insults, but to project and enunciate this time. So I walked on. Following me soon turned into chasing me. After about a mile, in an expanse of undeveloped land across from my house, I

---

31 Oh, what a difference a Skidoo ride makes with the pungent Kevin, upon whom Debbie apparently had a crush. Or, it was something else; I will never know. While some of us need to work through conflicts ASAP and openly, others, e.g. Debbie, want you to go through the rest of your life wondering what you did to offend them.

stopped running. I was out of breath, and felt I was owed an explanation. I shouted, "Why are you doing this?"

Nyanyoonyenyis? mocked Debbie. They had caught up with me, two against one, although Belinda seemed to be mainly a bystander. Debbie reached out and thumped my shoulder hard with the butt of her hand. I took a step backwards and sat down in a snow drift. This response took all three of us by surprise. It wasn't like Debbie had actually propelled me to the ground. My traitorous body had just gone into deferral mode all on its own. They looked down at me. Belinda scoffed or perhaps sneezed. Debbie kicked a chunk of ice in my direction, then—nonplussed by my passive acceptance of the situation, I suppose—the two of them left, strolling with triumphant slowness down the street together, arm in arm, to Belinda's house.

Watching them retreat, I felt I might combust. Did I spring to my feet and go after them? I did not. I waited until they were safely thumb-sized at the end of the block. Only then did I haul myself up and brush myself off. Adding pathos to my defeat, my lower half was now cold and wet. There was no language fitting my state of mind that I was authorized to use, so I made sounds that approached but did not fully realize cuss words: *Ffff! Shhh!* In this manner, I seethed my way home, after which I did something I would feel bad about for the next...well, I *still* feel bad

140

about it (or rather, conflicted: defiant, but ashamed). I went to the phone table, got out the phone book and looked up Belinda's family phone number. I dialed and waited while it rang. Now is not the time to explain life before texting—I have divagated enough—but you can Google *rotary phone*. Belinda answered politely, as we were all taught to answer the phone back then. "Baker residence, Belinda speaking."

I wasn't mad at her, per se. Nevertheless—not having thought things through, and teetering on the brink of an expressive collapse—I failed to request that she put Debbie on the line. I had a practiced cockney accent, and I wasn't afraid to use it. I did this so Belinda wouldn't be able to identify her caller. "You're stupid and ugly," I started in (*Yoh stewpih' an' ogly* is how that came out) "and everybody hates you (*ites ye*)."

Recalling this now, I'm so thankful that cyber-bullying had not yet been invented, or I would definitely have posted something public and deeply regrettable. Instead, only one person was exposed to my vitriol, and she didn't even really deserve it. "I hope all your clothes fall off at school!" I added. Having all your clothes fall off at school was the worst disgrace I could think of.

For some reason, she didn't hang up on me. That, I will never understand. Was she wondering *Who could this possibly be?* Was she waiting to hear everything I had to say? If so, she deserves what she got, just for being thick. I crescendoed with flair: "YOU STINK LIKE ARMPITS!" This was untrue, as—like every other girl—Belinda reeked of Herbal Essence shampoo.

For my finale, I slammed the receiver so wrathfully into the cradle that it cracked. For which I would get in trouble. Telephones were not ours to ruin; they were on loan from Ma Bell. Not only were Goodwins not the kind of people who let our feelings get out of control, we were definitely not the kind of people who destroyed somebody else's property. And of course, beyond the identity issues were the financial ones: this would be an unnecessary expense, one we couldn't easily afford. My mom's jaw set, she kept her mouth clamped shut against the admonishments I deserved. Which was worse, maybe, than hearing them. I was grounded for a couple of days, during which I grappled with what felt like both justice and injustice. Mom did not know the whole story. If she had, I might have rightly been made to apologize—*me! To Belinda!*—which, quite honestly, would have done me in.

I have revisited the sequence of events many times over the years. Because it's mystifying. Why didn't I: 1) not sit down in the snow, and 2) push back? I was unlikely to have caused the robust Debbie to slightly adjust her stance, but I would have communicated *Don't mess with me!* If they'd come at me for real then, all slappy and scratchy—so what? Worse than anything Debbie and Belinda might have done to me was the fury, the uncontainable fury, that—too late to do a bit of good—had risen up and destroyed something in my own house.

Little Red Cap and her grandmother, as everyone knows, are cut free, alive and well, by a huntsman, but in the Grimm story—a twist with which you might not be familiar—it is not the huntsman but she, Little Red Cap, who *kills* the wolf. She fills the empty cavity from which she has been liberated with large, heavy stones, and, unable to flee, he dies.

I wonder, how do you think Red would tell the tale? Would she say that she was victimized and traumatized, that she'd learned something about wolves, that she'd learned something about herself, that she would never trust again, that she was smarter and stronger for the experience, that this story would define her for the rest of her life? Would she say her story did not even matter, in a world where other girls, not so lucky as she, had been devoured whole and never seen again? Would she forget the story altogether, its importance diminishing as her life went on and other, better and worse things happened?

———————

I'm interested in the dos and don'ts, the shoulds and shouldn'ts that have contributed to my sense of me in the world, and taught me how to comport myself; in the messages I received since infancy (from church, books, television, and movies; from teachers and playmates) that girls ought to be pleasant and agreeable, boys will be boys, adults are to be obeyed, and most people can be trusted. I am also intrigued by all the moments in my life where, looking back now, I can see that I might have done something other than what I did (which may or may not have affected the outcome) but didn't, in part because those messages had so effectively disabled my wariness, my self-preservative instincts, my aggressiveness.

Why did I sit down? Why didn't I push back? One answer is that which I have already given above, and it both absolves and satisfies me. Another is that these encounters were in some way fortifying, as in *That which does not kill us*—yada yada yada.

What happens to and around us doesn't make us who we are, but how we reflect upon and make sense of it should tell us something about ourselves. One characteristic of my psychology is that I feel better about a difficult or ugly situation when I understand, acknowledge, and accept not only what happened, but my own role in its unfolding. More often than not, I approach my life and autobiography with curiosity. I am not boasting about this; I feel lucky that, on the whole, I tend to be inquisitive more than outraged—and lucky, too, that nothing so awful has befallen me it has shaken me beyond the capacity of curiosity to redress.

Not even this, which happened after Al, but before Shmed: When I went off to Boston for the very first time, in the fall of 1977, it was on my own, without my hardworking parents—one a teacher, the other a nurse—who would have certainly accompanied me, but I had begged to be allowed to travel on my own. At eighteen, I believed I was mature enough to handle the trip, and I'd convinced them that this was true. I was to check into my Newton campus dorm—BC's freshmen were housed two miles away from the main campus—on a Thursday morning. Long distance arrangements had been made for me to spend the night before at the home of a stranger, the East Coast friend of a Wyoming friend who, I'd been told, lived within a few hours of the school, and who had offered to put me up.

My host's name was Chris. He picked me up at the airport as per an agreement made via an exchange of letters. He turned out to be older than me—by a lot—and lived on his own in a little house. My parents had no idea about any of this, for I had assured them—though I possessed no information whatsoever beyond a phone number and an address—that I had checked out the whole situation, that it was on the up-and-up, and that I'd be perfectly safe.

Shortly after we got to his place, Chris had a number of pals over, six guys in their twenties and thirties. They turned up the stereo, drank and drank (I tentatively sipped a Miller Lite), and urged me to dance for them. This I halfheartedly ended up doing—even though *ick*—mostly because it seemed playful enough, and also because they were insistent: it got to the point where, by not dancing, I was clearly hurting their feelings, including the feelings of my host to whom I was beholden. I waved my arms, waggled my shoulders, swayed and hopped around, then excused myself—I was sleepy from my travels, and excited about tomorrow—so I lay down, still wearing my clothes.

Chris had made up the sofa with floral sheets and a comforter. He knelt beside me. "We're going to be playing cards here for a while and it'll be loud. Take these and they'll help you fall asleep." He handed me two pills and a glass of water. Because he seemed to care whether or not I slept well, and because it would have been rude to refuse a kindness, I took the pills and closed my eyes. When I opened them one second later, it was the next day.

146

Chris wasn't up yet. The house was quiet, the mess from last night—cards, ashtrays, beer bottles—littering the dining room table and floor. The place stank. My lower back and legs felt wet. I thought I'd maybe peed in my sleep, distressing enough, but when I reached my hand down, I realized I wasn't wearing my jeans. My hand came back covered in blood. I was mortified: I had apparently—it was the only explanation—undressed myself in my sleep, and my period had started ten days early. I had totaled Chris's sheets and—*Oh, no!*—his couch.

I rolled up all the bedding, not knowing what else to do, and turned the couch cushions upside down. I crept into the bathroom and scrubbed the sheets as I showered, but the huge bloodstain wouldn't lift out. I created a maxi-pad for myself from toilet paper (I hadn't brought any supplies, planning to buy what I needed after I got settled in Boston) and got dressed. I rolled up all the wet bedding and stuffed it into a hamper, wrote *Thank you so much!* on the back of an envelope, and left it, along with the only extra money I had ($20, which was to have been my emergency fund for my first month away from home) on Chris's coffee table. I hoped he could buy new sheets and that, somehow, he wouldn't discover the ruined furniture. I packed up my things, sneaked guiltily out the front door, and lugged my suitcase to the train, where a

Good Samaritan helped me figure out how to get where I wanted to go.

I continued to bleed. When I got to campus, checking into my dorm for the first time and joining the other excited freshmen, I had to repeatedly go to the restroom to replace the makeshift pad, which new ones I kept soaking through every twenty minutes. This was the worst period I'd ever had by far, but I wasn't concerned about it, just aghast at my body's betrayal of me. Why now, when I wanted to be happily meeting new people, making a good first impression and starting my new life as an undergraduate?

There was no one yet in my assigned dorm room, so I chose a bed, covered myself with a blanket and fell asleep for perhaps half an hour. I was awakened by the arrival of a throng: my new roommate, Paula*, and her entire family—parents, brothers, and sisters. I could feel that I'd bled through my jeans and onto the bed, so I kept myself covered as they gleefully crowded the room with suitcases, boxes, laughter, and plans to go out to dinner. They invited me, but I couldn't rise from the bed without revealing my situation, so instead shyly requested that they leave the room. I got up and changed. I didn't know what to do about my gory clothes or the mattress, so I turned the latter over, stuffed the former underneath it, and joined the group in the dorm's lounge. I was headachy, but did my

148

best to keep up my end of the conversation, to let Paula know she wouldn't be sorry to have me as her roommate.

That was how I started college. And for the next twenty-five years, it did not occur to me what had really happened to me at Chris's house while I was "sleeping"—which means that for decades, whenever I'd looked back—which wasn't often—I had cringed at how I'd ruined Chris's sheets and sofa then slinked away, rather than more properly cringing at the *Thank You!* note and compensative money I'd left for him.

Having had, at last, my *AHA!* moment, I feel quite protective of eighteen-year-old me. I wish I could go back, to offer guidance. I might say, for example—without revealing any of the specific details or consequences[32]—something along the lines of *Do not assume everyone has your best interests at heart,* or *Do not be so friendly, open, and accommodating,* or *Be more careful walking alone in the dark,* or maybe *Do not swallow mysterious pills out of politeness.*

She wouldn't have heeded, I don't think. Because she felt strong and whole; because she embraced life's ventures, risks, and surprises, and because her enthusiasm for

---

32 —which you're not supposed to do, according to a lot of movies, as it messes with the universe—

experience was boundless. She would have gone on, in defiance of my counsel, to attend Shmed's event, and she'd have ended up in his apartment. She would have sniffed when he said *Sniff!* She'd have walked, by herself, on Santa Monica Boulevard to the bus stop, no matter how dark the way, because she loved the electricity of Hollywood at night, humming and glittering with possibility, and how creative that sense of possibility made her feel. Intrigued, she'd have answered Eddie Cadabra's audition ad—just as she would have gone on, with only two hundred dollars to her name, to travel around Europe at twenty-three. She would have lived, without a plan and without knowing how she'd make ends meet, in Paris.

She'd have applied to a conservatory program and gotten in, moved to New York, and toured the country, coast to coast, for a year with six other actors in a van. She'd have relocated two thousand miles because she'd fallen for someone, taken out a loan to pay for graduate school, spent months—even years—writing plays in spite of theater's diminished relevance and economic impossibility. She was not someone who would have changed simply because I sat her down for a talk about life that included tips and admonitions. In fact she would have asked *Who are you to tell me what to do and not to do?* and I'd have said *I'm you at sixty-one*, and she'd have said *Well, then, you're a sixty-one-year-old idiot, because if I do what you say, you won't be you,* and I'd have replied, after a thoughtful pause, *Oh.*

Perhaps I ought to think less about advising the young woman and imagine, instead, teaching the girl, the eleven-year-old, to recognize her own power in the situation. Training her, in her body, to turn and face, to stand firm, to push back in equal measure, and to not sit down in the snow.

Chapter 10

Petrified

I could begin anywhere: me, trapped, unable to move, on a ledge near the base of the Flatirons, or the time I fell out of the dentist's chair, or how Marie-do and I became friends, or at the log on the Chavez and Beaver Brook trail, out near Windy Saddle, one of our first hikes together. I could begin with our last hike together: me, clambering up the slippery rock face of a limestone declivity that ended in a precipice—a thirty-foot tumble, from my position, would conclude on the unfortunate side of its edge, far below, in the sea.

I could—and shall—begin with how we came to be there and allow all those other stories to introduce themselves when their time comes.

We had set out, that morning, from a Metro stop on La Canebière, Marseille's high street, which ascends from the harbor through the largely Muslim quartier of Noailles, its name a reminder of the hemp merchants and rope-makers who did business there in the Middle Ages. Marie-do, a Marseille native, had promised me a day of sightseeing, exploration, and discovery. It was March; the skies were blue, the temperature cool, and I was feeling good. I'd been told we were going to the Calanques, though I wasn't clear whether *Calanques* referred to the mountainous area we'd be crossing, the inlets I could see on Google Maps, the national park that encompassed both, or all of the above. I just knew that the word *calanque* had a lithic, metallic onomatopoeia to it that I liked (it is fun to say) and feared (it has the ominous sound of a rockslide).

It was just the two of us. I may have mentioned already that Michael prefers traveling intellectually to traveling actually, and that I do not mind taking off and going places by myself. We have an arrangement: I go where I want without pressuring him to come along; he stays home—working, blogging, reading, having dinner with all of our friends who like him better than they like me, and consuming a tremendous amount of war, heist, gangster, martial arts, zombie, spy, and Marvel Comics entertainments—and I agree to never disclose any of that, or other private information, in a book.

Anyway, so, my husband was in Denver, no doubt watching *Deadpool* with a bowl of Jiffy Pop and finger of Laphroaig on the TV tray beside him, and I was in Marseille, with Marie-do. She and I had taken the Metro to a bus, and the bus for perhaps twenty minutes more, through the ninth arrondissement, to its final stop at Boulevard Louis Pierotti in the La Cayolle neighborhood. We were let out at the corner of a sleepy residential street where, in spite of a reputation for gang activity, it seems like nothing much probably ever happens.

But it is, in fact, a portal. Like Lucy Pevensie pushing through the coats in Professor Kirke's wardrobe and finding herself dramatically elsewhere, you do not expect to start off walking down this conventional lane, surrounded by commonplace apartment buildings, garden walls, hedges, pine and mimosa trees, only to end up, four hours in the future, clinging to the side of a rock, over a sheer drop, waves crashing far beneath the soles of your Merrells as they frantically seek purchase.

Just so you can picture us, I was wearing my cobalt windbreaker; Marie-do, her aquamarine jacket. I sported my boonie hat; she wore a sensible hood. I'd forgotten my collapsible trekking poles, but she had her pair—which she'd never used or needed in Colorado, and might have only brought, on this occasion, for my benefit, since I'm slow-ish going uphill and positively measured coming down. Poles help me to stabilize myself, and to move at an

acceptable pace (acceptable if you don't need to get anywhere by a certain time). These we divvied up. We each
carried a day pack, in mine a fleece, energy bars, tooth-
picks, extra socks, a flask of tea and of course, my first aid
kit. In hers, she'd packed a water bottle and sandwiches for
two. Once I learned there would be sandwiches, I found it
hard to concentrate.

Half a mile down the road from the bus stop, the quartier dwindled to one last house, then to an unpaved drive
that widened to a parking area, where we skirted a boom
barrier beyond which cars could not go. I was ready to take
advantage of the rustic but convenient *toilette*, sit down at
one of the wooden tables, and enjoy our lunch before heading home. I almost said as much, but before I did, we passed
a sign welcoming us to the *Parc National des Calanques*, and
I realized that we hadn't yet started our hike.

Marie-do's name is short for Marie-Dominique and is pronounced *MAHridoh*, like the trill of a brook flowing over
pebbles. We first met when we sat next to one another,
for a year, on a committee at the university where we
were both assistant professors (I, in the communication
department; she, in biology). Ours was a group of faculty
and staff devoted to complaining about, assessing, and
coming up with labor-intensive, well-researched, and

156

masterfully-argued proposals for improving learning environments—proposals that gradually, inevitably, found their way upward to an administrator's *Deleted* file. While small, the committee was not conversational; when we convened, it was to get through an agenda, at the end of which process there were never any outcomes. There were few chances to get to know one another in that context.

I had, however, noted that Marie-do was spirited, responsive, and French. Having lived in Paris in my twenties, I wondered whether I could still hold up my end of a *conversation*.[33] I hoped to initiate one. I spent an entire committee meeting working out, in my head, how to say, "How about we blow this cracker stand and go grab a pint?" but I couldn't get past *soufflons ce stand de cracker* [34]—and besides, why would a Frenchwoman who spoke flawless English want to duck out for a French *chit chat*[35] with me?

Our moment came when I eventually rotated, figuratively speaking, into the role of department chair and we—new chairs and old, including Marie-do—gathered at the dean's foothills cabin for a fall picnic and orientation. I remember exactly what happened: I dared to speak to her

---

33 —which is how you say "conversation" in French.
34 —which doesn't mean anything in French.
35 —which is how you say "chit chat" in French.

in French; she was warm and receptive, and after that, we just kept talking.

Beneath an overhang, a trough had once been cut into the earth and lined with stone. It collected water, which trickled from a small, arched opening, and which looked foul, so I was surprised to hear the part it had played in the region's ethnic, cultural, and political history.

When anyone explains something to me in French at a normal rate of speech, I understand every other word or phrase and make up what might reasonably come between. Thanks to my hearing loss, I'm adept at making sense out of a porous sequence such as *Once upon a time...daughter... drink...happily ever after.* I gathered, from Marie-do, that this, the Fontaine de Voire, was a place with legendary and historical significance having to do with the marriage, millennia ago, of an Ionian boy and an indigenous[36] girl—the Phoecaeans landed in Ségobrigian country just as the Ségobrigian princess was choosing a mate, which ritual selection she would effect by offering water from this very spring to the lucky guy. She had chosen Protis, one of the Greeks, marking the happy union of Phocaean and Ségobrigian cultures and the founding of *Massalia,* or

---

36 —which, in the region of the Rhône, refers to Celtic tribes—

Marseille. All that, I caught—but I had to request that we switch to English anyway, as I could have sworn there was also something in there about golf, Gypsies, and a vacuum cleaner.

Not long after we passed the Fontaine, we came to a cave, its black maw terrifying and irresistible. Had this geological feature been located anywhere near my hometown, its entrance would have been strewn with the detritus of delinquency, experimentation, and indulgence: the charred remains of illegal campfires, crushed beer cans, the butts of joints and filtered cigarettes, and, of course, used condoms and their empty wrappers. But, unlike my compatriots, the French do not tend to sneak and lie their way through post-adolescence, slyly or guiltily concealing their smoking, toking, drinking, and groping. *Au contraire*, such pleasures are considered to be natural, and do not have to play out in the back seats of cars, in basements, abandoned structures, or dark, creepy holes. Theirs is, I would argue, a healthy approach to growing up, although one wonders if French teens—shrugging off as banal the juvenile behaviors Americans see as transgressive—miss out on the thrill of getting away with stuff.

At any rate, there was not a welcome mat of litter here, just damp earth, rivulets, and a few fallen sticks and branches. I made my way over them all to peek within.

When I was a couple of feet inside the opening, I thought I heard a faint but resonant snort from the unseen recesses. It ought to have crossed my mind, but had not, that mammals of a certain size and temperament are known to occupy caves. I didn't want to enliven our expedition this early on with my qualms—which, in any case, were likely to become more, not less, pronounced as the day went on—so I just backed out and quickly (I would even say nimbly, for me) rejoined Marie-do where she waited. For once, it was I who vigorously assumed the lead.

"Nothing in there to be worried about at all," I reassured my friend, though she hadn't asked, as I sprinted ahead.

Unlike the well-traveled trails in the Rockies with which I am familiar, this was nonstop, ankle-breaking rubble, hard going that demanded attention to each step. Without incident or injury, we made it to a high, white ridge and stopped to gaze back at the valley from which we'd just come. By my estimate, we had been ascending the relentlessly stony trail for seventeen hours.[37]

Then, as we rounded a curve that led to the south side of the massif, an azure line appeared at the far edge of the world, the sea. Maybe—as a Westerner, one brought

---

37 —which Marie-do adjusted to forty-five minutes.

up with the cultural narratives that constitute the social construction of *Western-ness*—the closer one gets to the cradle of Western Civilization (this was the closest I'd ever been), the greater one's sense of *déjà vu*. Or else, I was hungry; either way, I felt swoony. I had pictured this landscape from childhood—probably first made aware of it at my mom's knee, when she'd read *Aesop's Fables* to me, or in elementary school when we had learned about the ancient Greeks and Romans. The spot where we stood was a palimpsest of myths, peoples, and cultures, and memories not my own, yet which seemed to belong to me.

So pellucid was the sky that, absurdly, I wondered if we could see all the way to Algiers. There were plenty of places to stop and take it all in. At the top of a scarp, we found a shelf, a fine spot for our picnic. Settling in, I heard another brutish grunt from somewhere among the pines, at which Marie-do introduced me to the brand-new information that there were wild boars all over the effing place.

"They do not usually attack," she added.

When Marie-do's husband, Mike, died a few years ago, back in Denver, it was not unexpected—young and athletic, he'd nonetheless been ill for a long time—but, it was sad. There's not much we can do to allay the pain of our important losses; grief, as far as I can tell, does what it wants with us, as it wants, when it wants, for however long it wants. Marie-do took time away from former routines to start new ones. She planted an abundance of flowers and vegetables in her yard. She planned a community garden for a church. She began biking, solo, for long distances. When she could bear it, she went through her and Mike's things, deciding what to keep and what to let go. She got herself outdoors, up into the mountains at every opportunity. The couple had enjoyed an active partnership, hiking, climbing, cross-country skiing, and snowshoeing, and now, she craved wilderness and the resistance and release that only rugged terrain can give our bodies and souls.

As our deepening friendship coincided with this period of heartbreak and transition, I was the fortunate beneficiary of Marie-do's love for nature and her willingness to share her time and hiking expertise with me. And she was the beneficiary of my mountaineering inaptitude, my laggardly pace, and my reluctance to push beyond mild physical discomfort. Now, I had never boasted along the lines of *Where I'm from, we live hard and we play hard* or *Danger is my middle name*, but nor had I warned her about my thimble-sized bladder, weak knees, and other noteworthy limitations. Marie-do had found out about them over time, and had also become acquainted with my heightened sense of risk (which I wish I could say I have exaggerated here for effect, but that would be a fib).

On the Chavez and Beaver Brook trail—not far outside of Denver—near the end of a four(ish)-mile trek, I balked at a waterfall crossing, which is to say a ten-foot log spanning an unremarkable cascade that, to me, appeared treacherous. Marie-do had just sauntered over it without even noticing that she was walking on a log, but I stalled behind her, staring at the plunging creek, imagining carnage: I would lose my footing. I would fall in. For how long, I wondered, would my shattered, drowned body— trapped inaccessibly among the rocks, leaves, and other debris—waft in the current before Search and Rescue arrived, tragically too late?

I looked into the cataract, then at Marie-do's genial countenance, the last face I would ever see. There was nothing to be done: she had crossed. I was on this side and must follow.

I stepped aside to allow a group of teenagers, a family with three small children, and a man with a prosthetic leg to proceed ahead of me, then took a deep breath and scuttled across.

A long time ago, in Amherst, Massachusetts, at the house on Stony Hill Drive where Michael and I lived while I was in graduate school, I was preparing to go to campus. I sat on the couch, bent over to tie my shoe, and tumbled forward like a sack of potatoes, landing on the rug.

A mental check of all systems established that I didn't feel sick. I was conscious and thinking clearly, yet I couldn't make it to my feet. Michael had left for work an hour earlier, and this was one of his Boston days, so he'd be halfway across the state by now. I crawled to the phone and called 911. "I don't know what's the matter," I reported, "but I've fallen, and I can't get up." In spite of the circumstances, hearing those words came out of my mouth, I giggled, after which involuntary outburst I had to convince the switchboard operator that this was not a prank call but an emergency.

I affirmed that no, I had not been drinking (*Never before nine in the morning,* I assured her); that I did not suffer from any known underlying conditions; that I wasn't hurt; and that yes, I was alone. In no time (Amherst is a small town) I was crawling to the door to let in two jovial EMTs. By the time they'd helped me to a chair, asked me a few questions, and checked my vital signs, I felt like an idiot, as I was now able to stand on my own and, but for a lingering sense of unreality, seemed fine. "Uh—" I offered, as they were departing, "I have no explanation for any of this, but thanks for coming."

"Good luck," said the short one.

I taught my freshman public speaking class, met with my dissertation advisor, and went to see my dentist for a regular checkup which went fine, right up until—after twenty minutes in a reclining position with my head tilted back—I was returned to upright, and things went intensely wonky.

WHOA! I shouted, at which everybody within earshot—patients, assistants, and the dentist himself—retreated, leapt to their feet, or gripped their armrests. *WHOA!* I repeated at the same decibel level, because I was at the revolving hub of a merry-go-round being pushed too fast. The room whirled. In trying to make it stop, I spiraled out of the chair, across the room and to the floor which, for a weird instant, I interpreted as being the ceiling. Like that morning, I was awake and alert—and now, deeply discomposed—but at least I hadn't damaged myself, somebody else, or any of the expensive equipment into which I might easily have face-planted.

The receptionist (no doubt having heard the commotion all the way up in the front office) had called for an ambulance. Within moments, two jovial EMTs spun into view.

"Hi again," I said, feeling bad that I was putting them through this twice in the same day. "I need to go to Cooley

Dick." Even though it sounds like more of my jokey non-sense, that is what locals—with a straight face—call the hospital, which is officially named Cooley Dickinson.

"Perfect," said the tall one, strapping me onto a gurney, "because that's where we're going." I hoped they weren't taking me to the psych ward.[38]

After lunch it was all downhill, literally speaking, and talus the whole way. I made fairly good time, motivated by the prospect of chancing upon a mad pig with tusks. When, finally, we emerged from a long stretch of woods, it was onto a wide beach where the Mediterranean met the calcareous shore. Wind thrashed up the waves, flapped at our jackets, and whipped our hair.

"Wow," I said, and meant it. Behind us were the mountains we'd descended; ahead of us, along the coast, a trail that stretched away to the west, meandering over rock weathered by the ages, its surface rough in some places, smooth and polished in others. A few people could be made out, mere dots, moving along it. I was beat, com-pletely done in. My hips and legs felt like concrete, if concrete could be sore. I looked around for the bus stop,

---

38 I'm not saying I've ever been on a psych ward. I have not, so who am I to not want to be taken to one? I'm sure they are perfectly nice places. Please, don't assume that I am anti-psych ward and cancel me.

but there was nothing resembling a road, or—except for a small restaurant, which apparently could only be reached by boat—any other signs of civilization.

"We are going way over there," Marie-do pointed to the distant horizon where the pale, hilly land met the sea. "Around this calanque, then around another one, and then around the last one."

Nobody had an explanation for my condition. I was medicated with meclizine. As Michael was still in Boston (I hadn't had a chance to phone him, and now felt it was unnecessary since I wasn't dying or even being admitted) a friend collected me at Cooley Dick and drove me home. I listed my unsteady way into the house...and for the next three weeks got around by holding onto walls or Michael, whose upper arm developed clutch bruises.

I underwent tests. In Boston, a team of specialists encircled me and pushed me back and forth, trying to tip me over like a roly-poly doll. I thought I might have mistakenly entered the wrong office, not Otolaryngology but The Ministry of Silly Diagnostic Procedures. In spite of the hilarity, they were unable to come up with anything except the obvious: I was dizzy.

A lesion was discovered in my inner ear on the right, my deaf side, but nobody could say with any certainty whether that was the cause of the trouble. Could be migraines or Meniere's, though experts disagreed on this, eventually rejecting those guesses.

And then, nobody cared. When doctors cannot figure out what is wrong with you after a certain amount of effort, they assume you're a whiner and begin using their indulgent, dismissive voices when answering your insistent questions. They want you to stop bothering them.

When at last, one fine day, I woke up and felt like my old self again, it was no thanks to the medical community. My restoration, I supposed, was a matter of enough time having passed. Maybe I'd had a weird virus.

The inner ear is a labyrinth. Hundreds of millions of years ago, the earliest animals developed in aqueous environments where it was essential that they be able to feel the flow of the water around them. Descended from these predecessors who were first able to sense movement and rotation, humans have, deep in our ears, what are called semi-circular canals. These are filled with fluid and lined by hair cells composed of superfine cilia, which evolved as motion sensors and which help us to experience up, down, and other directions, and to stay balanced. Microscopic crystals—otoconia or otoliths—"ear rocks"—consisting of calcium carbonate, the material from which the mountains and cliffs of the Calanques are also made—are piled atop the hair cells, stuck there by a gel layer. When our heads tilt, the crystals shift, and that is how we orient to gravity. Sometimes, due to any number of factors ranging from congenital malformations to disease to trauma, a clump of crystals comes loose and falls or floats into a semicircular canal—a rockslide, if you will. This can result in vertigo, possibly severe, during which your body has no way of knowing where it is in space, and things around you seem to spin.

One night in 2016, after no issues for years, I rolled over in bed the wrong way[39] and ended up in the emergency room at Denver's St. Joseph Hospital. Michael tried to steer me as I careened across the vast lobby. I was still in my pajamas and robe because I'd been unable to get dressed. In between my paroxysms of profanity—which I should have tempered, given the full waiting area—we attempted levity: Michael wanted to know if he should make it clear to the triage nurse that I am not usually a ringer for Bill the Cat. I said *Yes, please*, then threw up in a trash can.

---

39 Seems, doesn't it, that the older you get, the more there is a wrong way to do everything, including sitting, sleeping, and breathing.

The attending physician knew his stuff. Unlike the befuddled doctors in Massachusetts who had never seen or heard of anything like my complaint, this one instructed me through a series of facilitated moves he referred to as the Epley Maneuver. He had me turn my head to the affected side. As all of reality felt like the affected side, it took us a miserable interval to determine which directional movements most exacerbated the spinning.

Then I lay down. The doctor eased me back, looked into my eyes, and pronounced *nystagmus*—which, Michael and I soon learned, means that your eyeballs appear to be cartoonishly circling in your head. Subjectively, you're riding the Tilt-a-Whirl. When this hell subsided, he turned me over, watched my eyeballs flicker rapidly from side to side again, then sat me up.

What I have loosely described is one of several procedures that can be done to reposition canaliths, the rocks in one's head. The spinning sensation decreases when those pesky, errant crystals have drifted out of the semicircular canals, where they do not belong and should not be allowed. So first of all, *hallelujah* for the maneuver's innovator, one John Epley of Oregon. And, second of all, why had none of the doctors I'd seen in Massachusetts known about this maneuver—which, according to the attending physician, was not Top Secret but standard procedure for what seemed to be a simple case of benign positional vertigo?

"Benign," I pronounced, tentatively relieved. "That sounds all right, then."

"Yes, well, it's horrible—but, unless it happens when you're in a precarious position, it won't kill you."

I was not supposed to lie flat or crane my neck, and I should be prudent, too, when looking down.

Just try, Michael paraphrased, *to keep a level head.*

Regarding the path that extended the length of a polished limestone strand, Marie-do first cautioned, "Be careful; it gets wet and can be slick" then, "Be careful; it's really windy," and last of all, remembering something else up ahead, she said, "Uh-oh."

Over the course of the twelve or so hikes we'd completed in Colorado, not to mention the many drinks, dinners, and walks we'd enjoyed together, Marie-do and I had covered more metaphorical than geographic ground. From teaching and the institution of education to love, family, and faith; from the purpose of collecting primate scat in Costa Rica (her project) to the crucial function of comedy in society (my favorite rant), our subjects were generally suggested by mutual curiosity about phenomena we'd observed, quandaries we'd faced, or questions we'd pondered. Early in our relationship, we'd recognized that we both preferred silence to politics, rumormongering, or griping. Often, for long stretches, we'd be quiet, moving at different speeds, Marie-do far ahead, me picking my way over the terrain. As we did now. After another hour and a half of bracing wind, glorious vistas, and the cautious placing of one foot before another—my body more strenuously worked than I could remember it having been in ages, my ligaments beginning to tighten, my joints to stiffen, and my glutes and quads to burn—I caught up with my friend as she considered what was coming up. The route would soon rise to where it disappeared around a bend, after which was what she characterized as our last leg. This was great news, as I was on mine.

"So what was the *uh-oh?*" I inquired.

"It's not a big deal," she said. "When we get there, we'll just do it."

The *it* we would *just do* when we got there turned out to be a short bit—no more than five or six yards—where the trail vanished, in its place a partially-denuded boulder, the only visible way beyond it being up, over it.

The place was magnificent. High atop the hill squatted an old military lookout house, the Sémaphore. Below were a pair of steep-walled coves. The slope we were on was angled maybe forty degrees, but our prospective, and apparently necessary, ascent would be steeper—steep enough that you would need to engage hands and feet; steep enough that gravity would not leave you where you landed, were you to fall. No, you would bounce, then roll down to—and over—the edge of the cliff below. This vividly unfolded in my mind's eye—including the flustered look on my face and my pinwheeling arms—and, while the whole thing was funny to watch, I hoped not to realize its slapstick potential.

Nothing in the surrounding terrain suggested an alternative way forward, or certainly not one that someone like myself would blithely undertake. My mouth felt impossibly dry, and partly because of that (but also to kill time) I pulled out my tea flask and took a swig.

What I was seeing was not the scene in front of me, but another one entirely: years ago, me and my brother, Mitch, at the base of the Flatirons in Boulder, following an easy trail one afternoon, not hiking to hike but only to spend time together. We were most definitely not out to challenge ourselves.

Through a bit of forest, we came to the base of a massive, red outcrop, more of an overhang, actually, where the path—which was somewhat crowded—ran atop a ledge that dropped perhaps fifteen feet to the floor of a ravine.

There was nothing here, really, to unnerve most people: you would walk single-file until you came to this one interruption—a spot where you'd have to turn sideways and inch along a bulge to continue on the other side.

Mitch was chatting, illustrating a finer point as he scooted along the wall and kept going. My arms out, I mimicked his position and got myself to where the bulge made any kind of compensatory crouching or bending impossible. I was suddenly aware of the empty space that yawned at my feet. I lost my center; I couldn't find within me that sense of a plumb line that tells our bodies how to stand upright and I gripped, or froze up. I don't mean I stopped; I mean that I turned to stone.

My brother realized that he'd been talking to himself. He turned around and retraced his steps to where I remained motionless, a crowd of other hikers gathered behind me trying to encourage me to either go on or to come back.

"It's not that I don't know what to do," I snapped crabbily at my audience. "I am not just being indecisive."

Mitch prompted me to come to him, but I was barely able to turn and look in his direction. From the spectator gallery, a man sidled over me, took the wrist he could reach, and yanked me gently but firmly to safety. Then, he and the crowd all clamored to know if I was okay which,

174

of course, I was except for the loss of dignity, and dignity is overrated: I have gotten along fine without very much of it.

Mitch and I sometimes laugh about that episode. But now, facing a similar challenge—knowing how my body had refused my commands on that and so many occasions—I wasn't feeling all that amused.

We had to determine whether Marie-do would go ahead or after. I saw no reason to take us both out when I plummeted, and besides I remembered, from our Beaver Brook crossing, the steadying sense of having her waiting for me at the other side of a difficult patch, smiling and holding out her hand. "You go," I said. "I'll be right behind you."

Within seconds of starting up, I understood what *exhausted* means. I wasn't able to move with any confidence or precision; my limbs felt torpid, though my heart was hammering. Then, halfway, I looked up at my endpoint, which I ought not to have done.

The movement of lifting my chin caused a lurch in my sense of earth and sky, gravity and weightlessness, equilibrium and disequilibrium. The weight of my pack, until now negligible, was at once a liability, tugging at my upper body. I heard myself wailing, whether in the privacy of my own thoughts or out loud, I cannot say.

During our descent from the heights, Marie-do had given me her trekking pole, and I'd continued to use both as we'd skirted the coast. Since, grappling now, I was unable to make progress with them in my hands, I thrust them up at Marie-do: "CAN YOU TAKE THEM? TAKE THEM! SORRY!" And even though she, herself, was not yet solidly-situated, she somehow incorporated both poles into her own climb. "THANKS!" I shrieked.

The blue sky reeled. I was not going to make it. Marie-do held out a pole, which I grabbed, and helped me up. As I sat, pulling myself together, the spinning subsided.

"Ça va?" asked Marie-do.

"Yep," I said. An octogenarian with a terrier on a leash passed us, heading in the opposite direction. "*Bonjour, mes-dames!*" she called out cheerily, sauntering over (and disappearing down and beyond) the boulder we'd just scaled.

I limped, Marie-do walked, around the last calanque, Callelongue, where, past the port, on the far side, a bus picked us up and transported us back to Marseille. During the half-hour ride, we said nothing. I stared out the window at the passing shoreline, the city's outskirts giving way to residential, then urban neighborhoods. The whole way, I thought about our day, appreciating the spectacular, unforgettable route my friend had chosen: we'd gone from

the birthplace of Marseille to the sea, around the calanques, and along the Corniche to the Old Port at the heart
of the city.

Getting off the bus, I staggered, barely able to stand
and positive that I would never make it up La Canebière
to the little apartment I was renting. Boats bobbed in the
water of the harbor, the far side of which was bordered by
a row of restaurants, brasseries, cafes, and bars, and all at
once, I didn't want the day to be over.

"Drink?" I suggested, which is not the wrong thing to
say at the conclusion of an adventure.

I don't think you can have an experience while also trying to document it. The penchant today for capturing the
moments of our lives so that we can *share* them—a word
I've come to dislike—is nothing less than alienation, a
way to distract ourselves from being fully present, alone
or with others, in the moments we're living. While we are
preoccupied with framing the here-and-now for later, for
our so-called *followers*, we cannot appreciate the unsettling
parts of solitude, the boring parts of being, the ignominy
of embodiment, or the meaninglessness of our activities.

Be that as it may, I SO regret not having a photograph
of me and Marie-do on that hillside, an image taken during
those few, harrowing seconds when I hung, or thought I

hung, over thin air. The next day, I drew and texted her this, which to me expresses a lot about my psyche, but which she rejected as inaccurate:

"This is awful," she declared. "Is that what you think happened?"

When she pointed out that she had not stood there watching me struggle with a smug expression on her face (my artistic failing, not my perception) I went back to the drawing board. Here is my second attempt.

You will note that in this one, Marie-do is leaning down to pull me up, that she appears to be appropriately concerned, that the angle of the boulder is somewhat more realistically-depicted, and that I am damned close to the edge of that thing.

For Marie-do, with love

Chapter 11

The End of the World Notwithstanding

I have a recurring nightmare. I'm in my room, only re-conceptualized by Alfred Hitchcock. I'm alone, but there is something in here with me. I can't see it, smell it, hear it, or touch it, but it's malicious. It is malignant. It has intentions. What keeps happening is: *nothing*. I can't take the suspense. I start punching at the air, bellowing at the top of my lungs, *BRING IT ON! YOU LAME-ASS, PISSANT DOUCHEBAG! COME AND GET SOME A ME! AAANGHHH!*

This wakes me up. My pulse is throbbing, my hands are empty, and I am so bummed out that I met with no resistance. That, when I tried to make contact with what I thought was there, it wasn't.

———

Yes, terrible things happen, most of them unrelated to anything I think is about to occur. If you missed that central moment in the tornado story and remain on the edge of your seat—*Hold on! Did that storm destroy the town of Otis and everyone in it?*—the answer is no, it did not. If what's left you hanging, instead, is the fire at Woods Landing (with which this book began, and the outcome of which until now has remained uncertain) I shall return to that—satisfactorily if not conclusively—in just a sec. And for you who cannot stop thinking about the Grand Canyon—*What was it, specifically, Janna, that blew your mind and changed your life? WILL YOU NEVER TELL US?*—I turn, in my journal, to page 78:

> Once inside Kaibab Forest, you come across spots to pull over that promise your first experience of the canyon. You stroll from the Desert View parking lot toward the Watchtower and the rim. Notice, returning to their cars—coming from where you're headed—people, walking past you in silence, whose faces are transfigured.

182

I contrast this sense of the holy with what I witnessed last time Michael and I were in France, visiting Notre Dame, a few years before the great fire of 2019. As you approached the cathedral, gazing up at its gargoyles, chimeras, and flying buttresses, you joined a horde of international tourists lining up, milling around the vast, stone plaza, waiting to enter. The Entitled, of whom the world has no shortage, made their way forward through a deft combination of determination, opportunism, and elbows. Those less inclined to claim a place of privilege—let us call them The Meek—were crushed in the middle, or retreated to the edges. If I admit to having been among the former, I'm an asshole. If I admit to having been among the latter, I'm a pussy. Nobody wants to be a pussy, so let's cut to the interior, to the sanctuary. Where in spite of shadowy transepts, lurking statues, looming arches, gleaming pews, distant murmurs and prayers—all of which might have at once humbled and elevated the spirit—what prevailed, instead, was the squeaking of sneakers, the clicking of cameras, and whispers of impatience: *MOM! MOM! CAN WE WAIT OUTSIDE? PLEASE? WE WANNA GO OUTSIDE.*

The Grand Canyon is different. For one thing, you are already outside. And here, unlike in the cathedral, people have been shut up by awe. From all over the world, carrying packs, maps, and water bottles, they pass, these brothers and sisters who have been changed by having seen what you are about to see. And then it is your turn, and you are there.

One response to your first time might be *Behold what the Lord made for us!* Or, alternatively—and this was my own thought, which I worked through with a park ranger who was stuck at his post and could not get away from me—"So! If I am accurately interpreting this geological testament to time and physics—" I made a sweeping gesture out and across, in case he didn't get what I was talking about "—then my entire life span and everything that's transpired during it amounts to not even a sentence in this text! A single character, perhaps?"

To which he replied, after giving it some thought, "Possibly a question mark while you're still alive. And then a period."

That night at the motel, I spent no time on the Lightship Columbia. I dropped off when my head hit the pillow. Woke in the morning to find a giant cockroach—couple of inches long—squished underneath me in bed, a nighttime visitor. The brown carapace. The wings. The antennae still feebly waving around. Without any wailing, gnashing of teeth, rending of garments, or tearing of hair, I picked it up and flushed it down the toilet. Preoccupied. I could

184

not wait to get back. To stand on the verge. To take in the glorious indifference of a universe that requires of me nothing—no apology, flattery, praise, pretense, or supplication—yet which stirs within me reverence, gratitude, and a sense of belonging to…well, to everything.

No, I did not go down inside the canyon. Why is that the first thing everybody wants to know? What am I, Indiana Jones? I drive a Fiat 500 named Vern! I use Nordic trekking poles in City Park! Why would anybody in their right mind, in one hundred two-degree heat, go down in there? There is at least one big, thick volume—*Over the Edge* is the evocative title—dedicated to all the different ways you can die at the canyon, and *going into it is the main way.*

I don't need to turn the Grand Canyon into a personal proving ground: me against nature, me against you, me against me. Instead, I can hike for miles along that precipice, taking it all in. Being there, in no contest with anybody or anything. Up top are pathways marked with arrows! Up top are descriptive plaques, protective railings, and sanitary facilities! When you grow hot and weary, a free, air-conditioned shuttle bus comes along, driven by a friendly retiree who encourages you, as you disembark at any of the scenic overlooks, to *Please enjoy the splendor of the Grand Canyon in whatever way you choose. Remember: your safety is your own responsibility. Watch your step and have a great day.*

All this is what I drove up here to think about—to Woods Landing, Wyoming, to this lovely hamlet, this normally tranquil spot where people gather to dance on Hokum Lestrum's sprung wood floor, and where today a force of nature blazes, out of control, a short distance away, threatening to annihilate. But look: it is already diminished, already submitting to the good, human, collaborative efforts to put it out.

Until I have to leave—should it come to that—I've got my Titan IPA, Nietzsche, my journal, my ukulele, and the five notes I can fingerpick. And I understand that what overwhelms, more often than not, isn't the fire, the snake, or the bully. Mostly, it's the imagination. The idea, the inconceivable thought that we will no longer exist, and so—did we ever? Who is going to be around in a billion years to say one way or the other? Nobody, that's who.

I don't matter. You don't matter.

Let us lift our cans and toast to that: *Oh, well—HA!*

Standing at Yaqui point at the end of the day, you gasp to catch your breath as the colors of those layers upon layers of time change, little by little, from sand to flame to ochre to night with the beating of your heart.

Every moment matters. It matters that I witnessed a woman's death that morning on Highway 50, and that I will not forget her. It matters that Oscar and I made eye contact for three long seconds, and that we knew what to say to one another. It matters that you miss your son. That you got the job. That the baby was born healthy…or not. That we are here together. It matters what happens next. What happens next? *Idunno.*

Chapter 12

Peaches

Before you go, I will tell you: you may suffer
You may cry
You may often feel afraid and you will ache in the pain
of confusion
You will taste honey from the field though you may
receive the sharp sting of the bee
I will not always be with you
I cannot always be watching
I'll not be able to prevent you from coming to harm
You may lose an arm, a leg, a hand, a tooth, an eye
You may lose one you love or many, many
But you will eat peaches. You'll see suns set
You will inhale the warm scent of grasses, of hyacinth,
of skin
And one day, the sharp spoke of the wheel will pierce
your heart

When all this torment, opposition, and the sweet sublime
    will dull to cold
In that tiny moment, as you're saying goodbye
I'll tell you now and then you decide
I promise you, you will want more
Truth is the light you never see
Truth is the light you never see
Truth is the light you never see 'til it's gone.

The End

Acknowledgments

The End of the World Notwithstanding was once a solo comedy performance, *You Are Reminded That Your Safety Is Your Own Responsibility*. For her part in the development of the script, I'm forever indebted to my director and friend, Lee Massaro. Thanks to the United Solo Festival in New York, the Marsh Theatre in San Francisco, VooDoo Comedy in Denver, The Nantucket Island School of Design and the Arts (NISDA), Kim Vasquez, Tara Robinson, Ethan Karson, David Hicks, Jon Richard, Regis University, and the colleagues and loved ones—too many to name—who endured in-progress stumble-throughs and pre-opening showings, and whose feedback helped to shape the telling of the original stories. To the friends and relatives who make cameo appearances in the pages that follow, love always. To the strangers herein, a little wave of greeting, and to the assailants and foes, a direct message: *You know what? I've had just about enough of you.* For their warmth, encouragement, support, and affectionate teasing, deep appreciation to my husband, my mother and father, and my brothers, Mitch and Matt. For faith in me and in the book, and for their editorial vigilance and guidance—one might, for instance, note what I hope is the consistent use of the serial comma throughout—thank you to James O'Reilly and Larry Habegger. The story of the fire at Woods Landing first appeared in *Defenestration* on January 22, 2020.

About the Author

Janna L. Goodwin grew up in Casper, Wyoming, briefly attended Boston College, dropped out to write music reviews and perform improv comedy in Los Angeles, lived in France, and studied theatre at the National Shakespeare Conservatory in New York. She co-founded Ko Theatre Works, then earned a BA in Film and Music from Hampshire College and a doctoral degree in Communication from the University of Massachusetts, Amherst. Her plays—including *Killing Andrea*; *Serving Time*; *The House Not Touched by Death*; *If You Lived Here, You'd Be Home By Now*; *Pointers*; and *Mother's Day*—have been produced by independent theatre companies on the East Coast and in Colorado. Her solo show, *You Are Reminded That Your Safety Is Your Own Responsibility*, premiered at the United Solo Theatre Festival in New York and provided the material for this, her first book. Janna is a professor in the Department of Communication and a playwriting mentor in the Mile High MFA program, both at Regis University in Denver, Colorado, where she lives with her husband, Michael Karson.